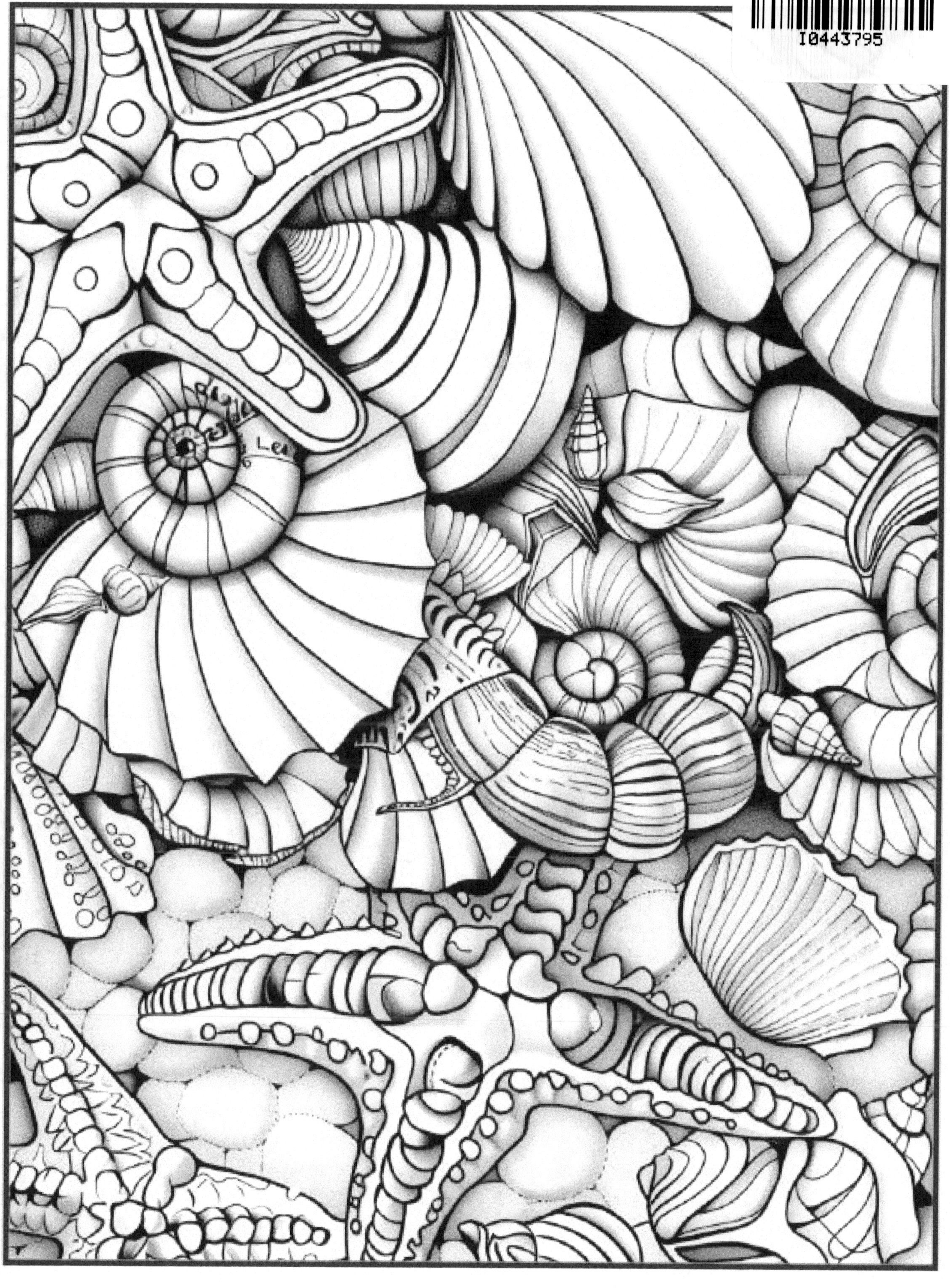

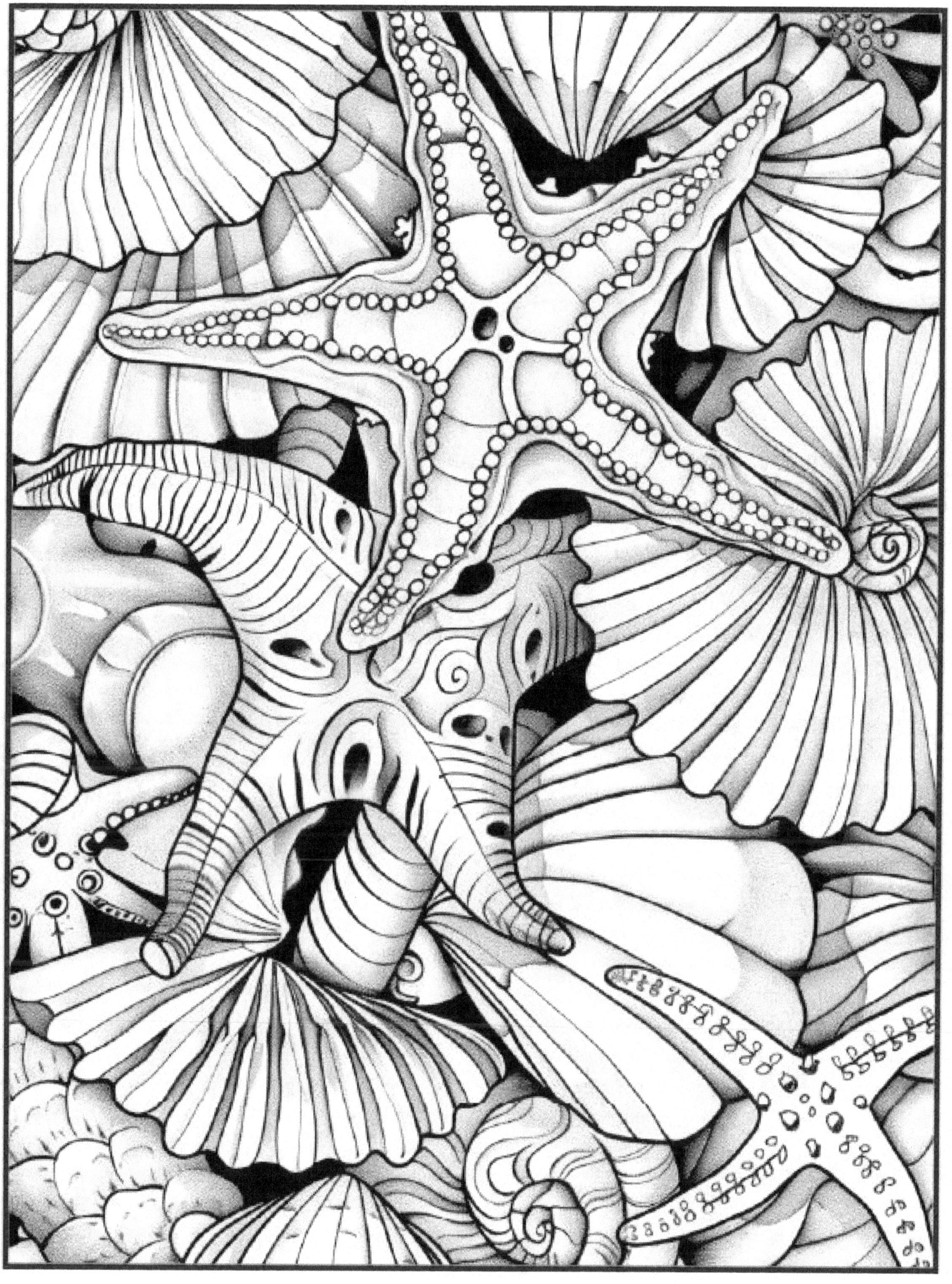

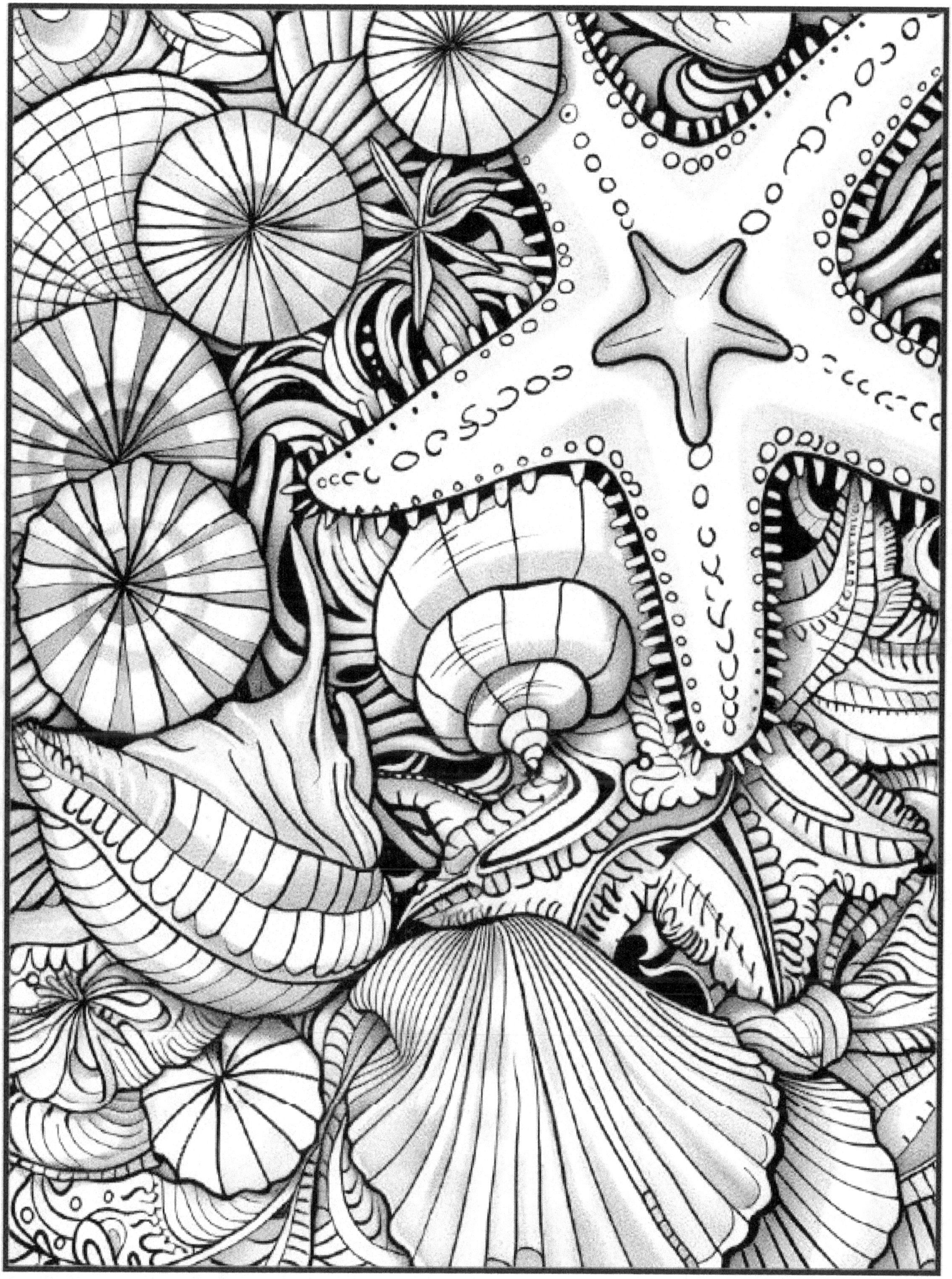

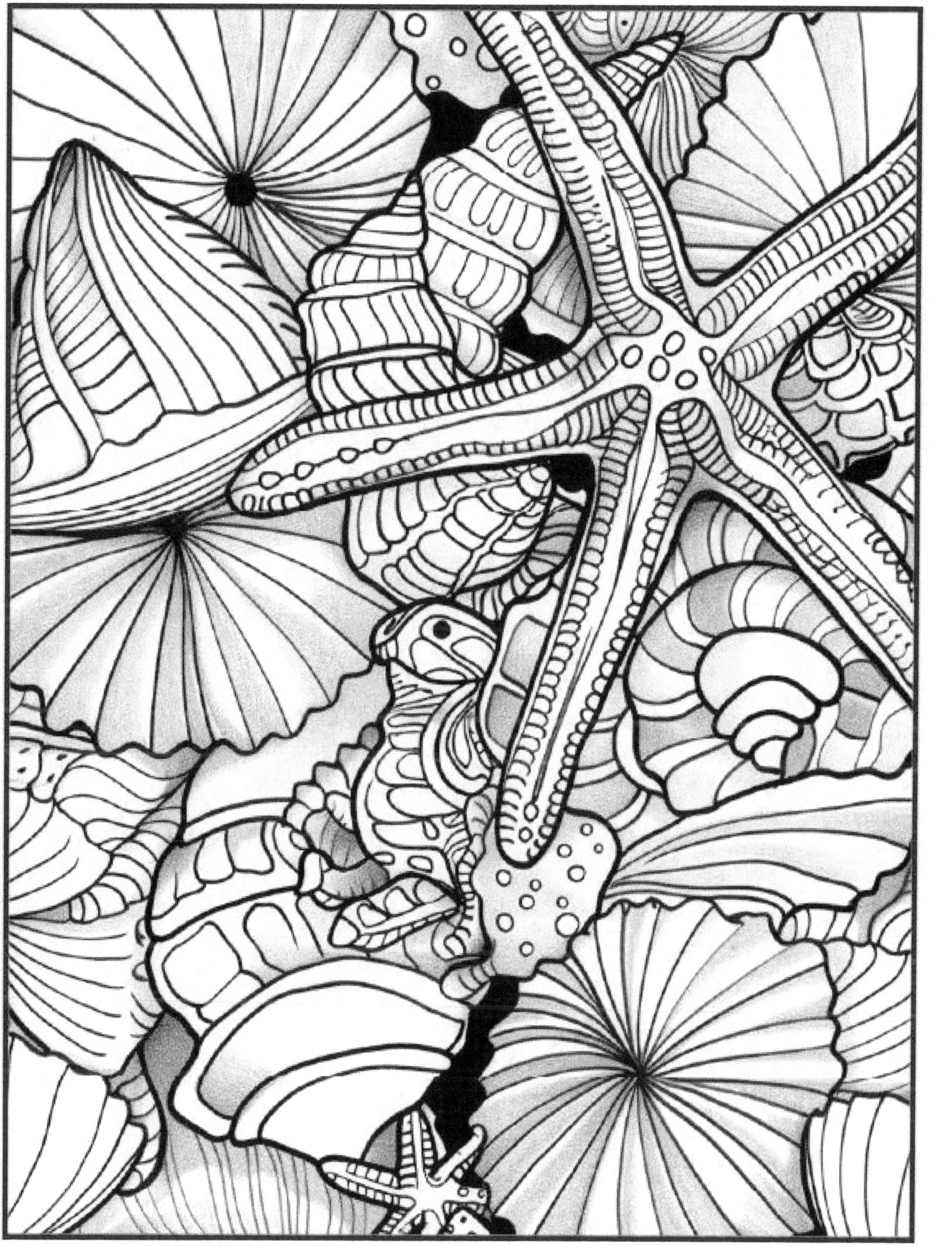

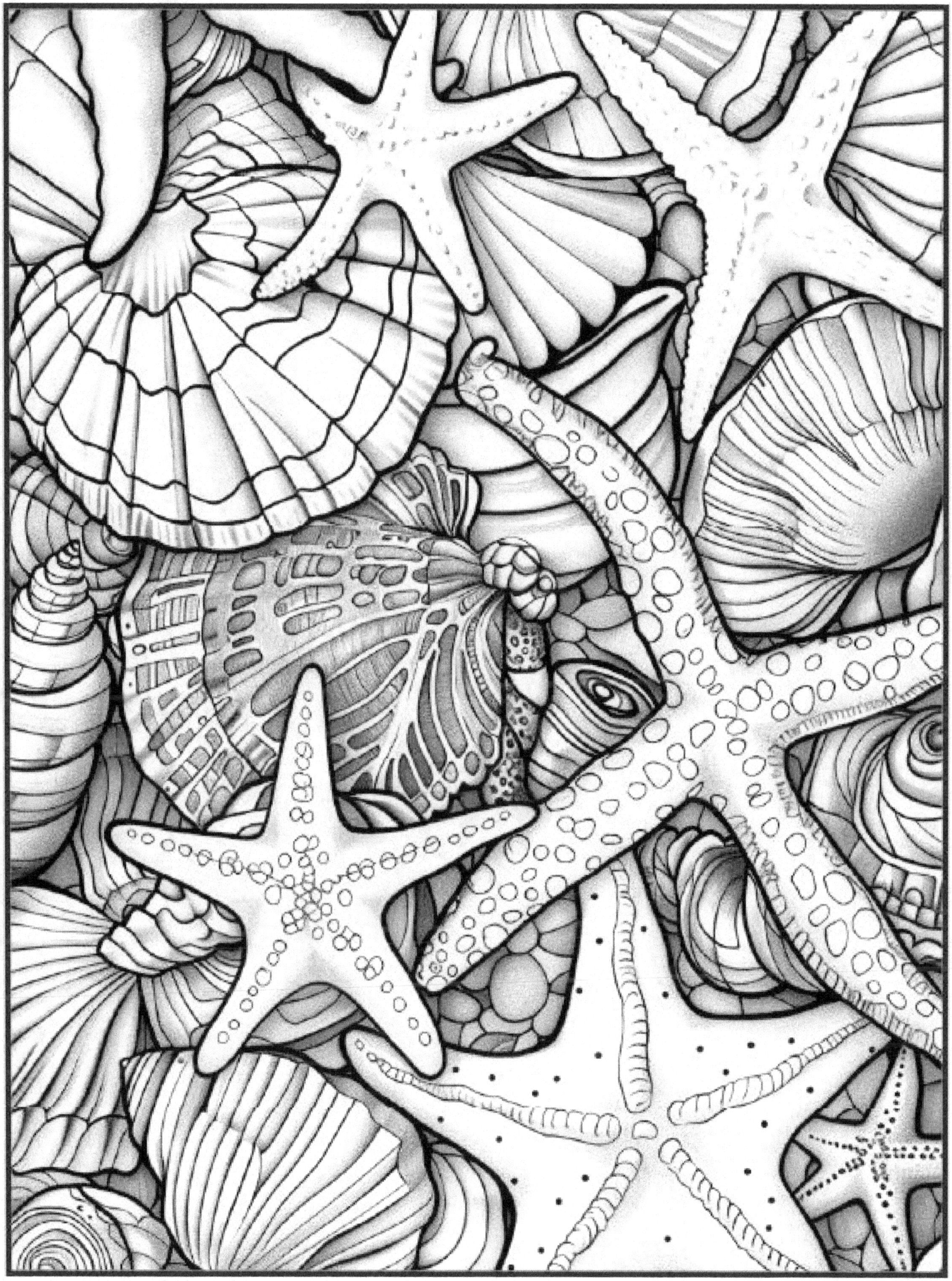

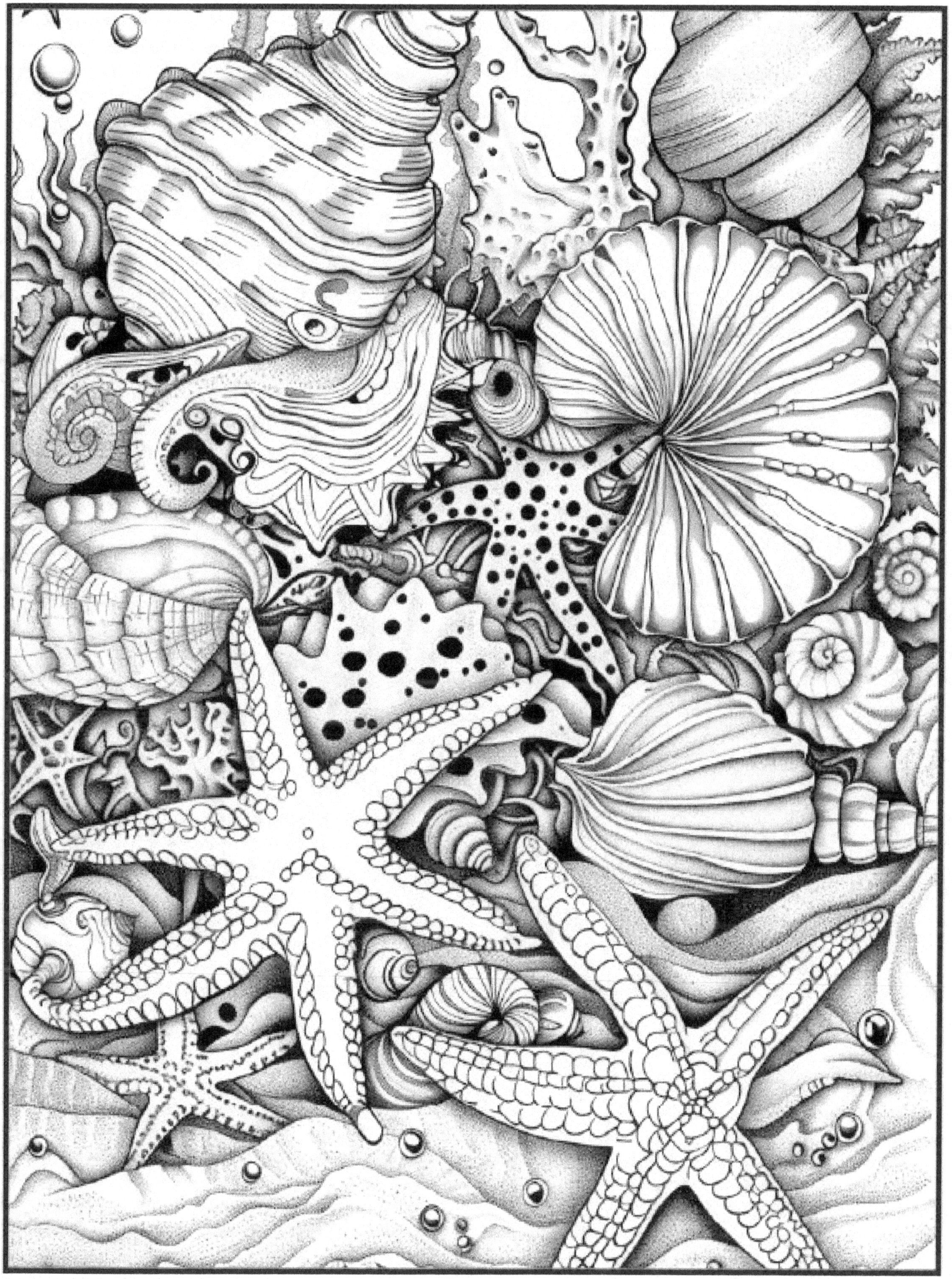

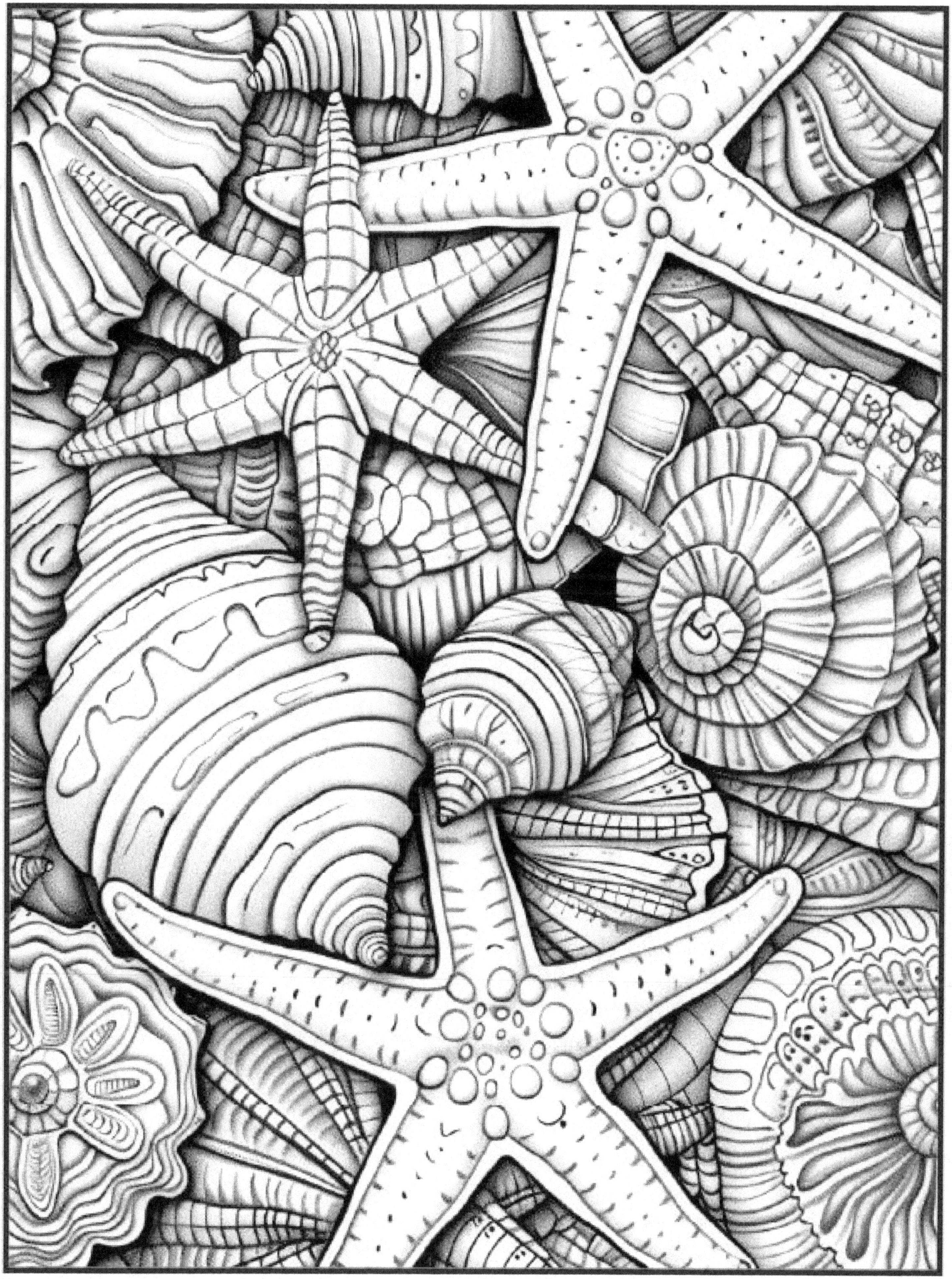

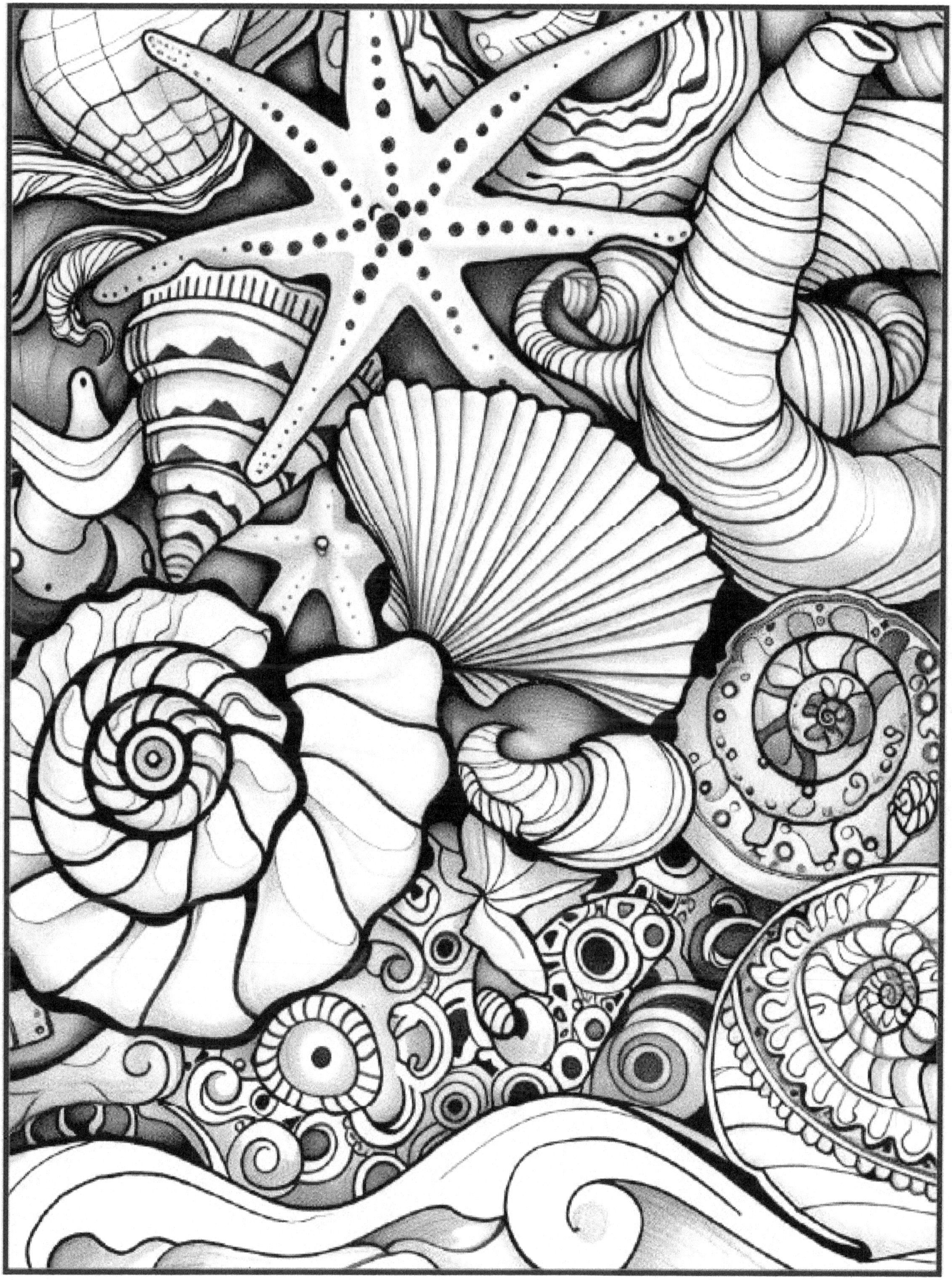

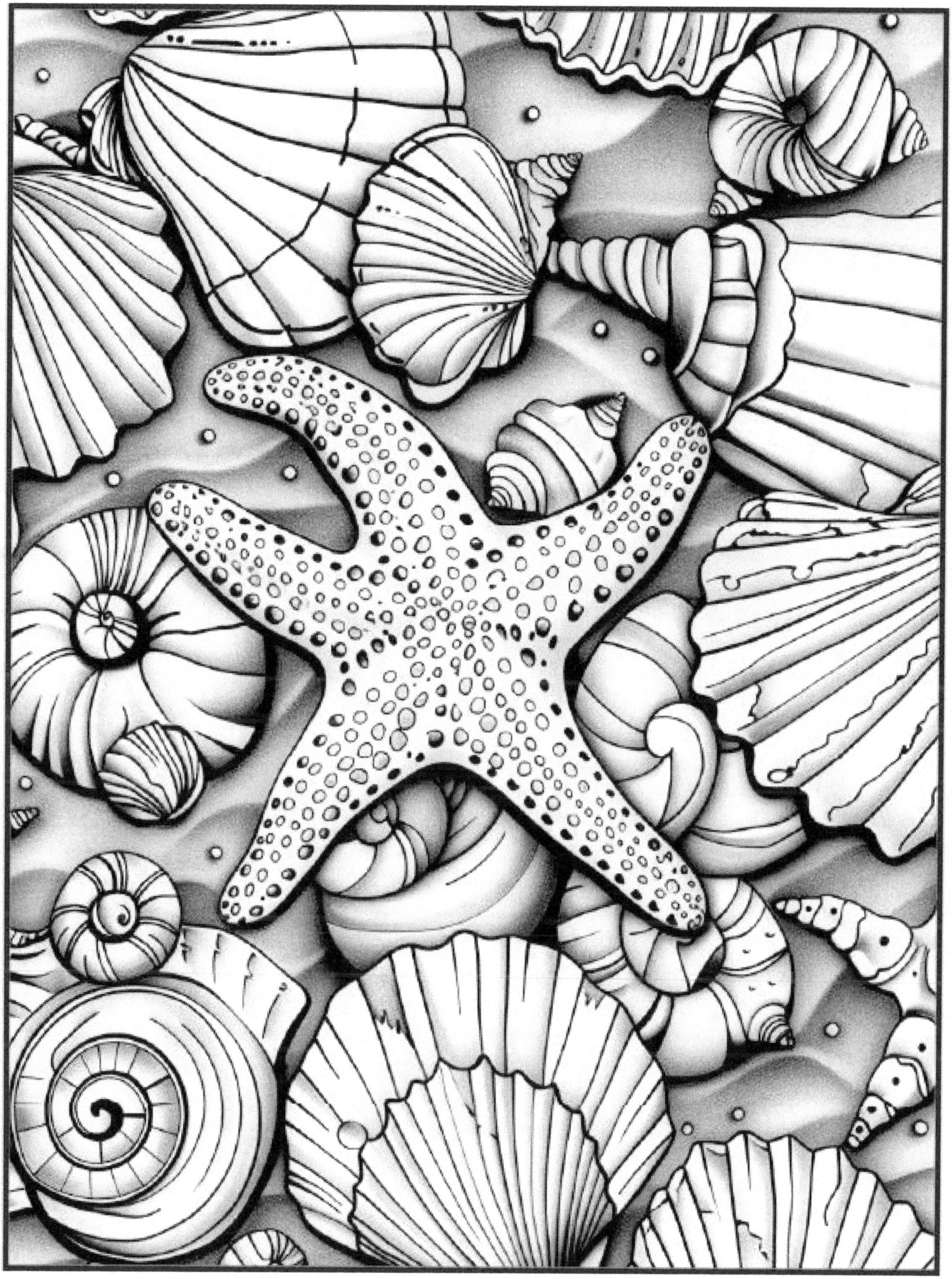

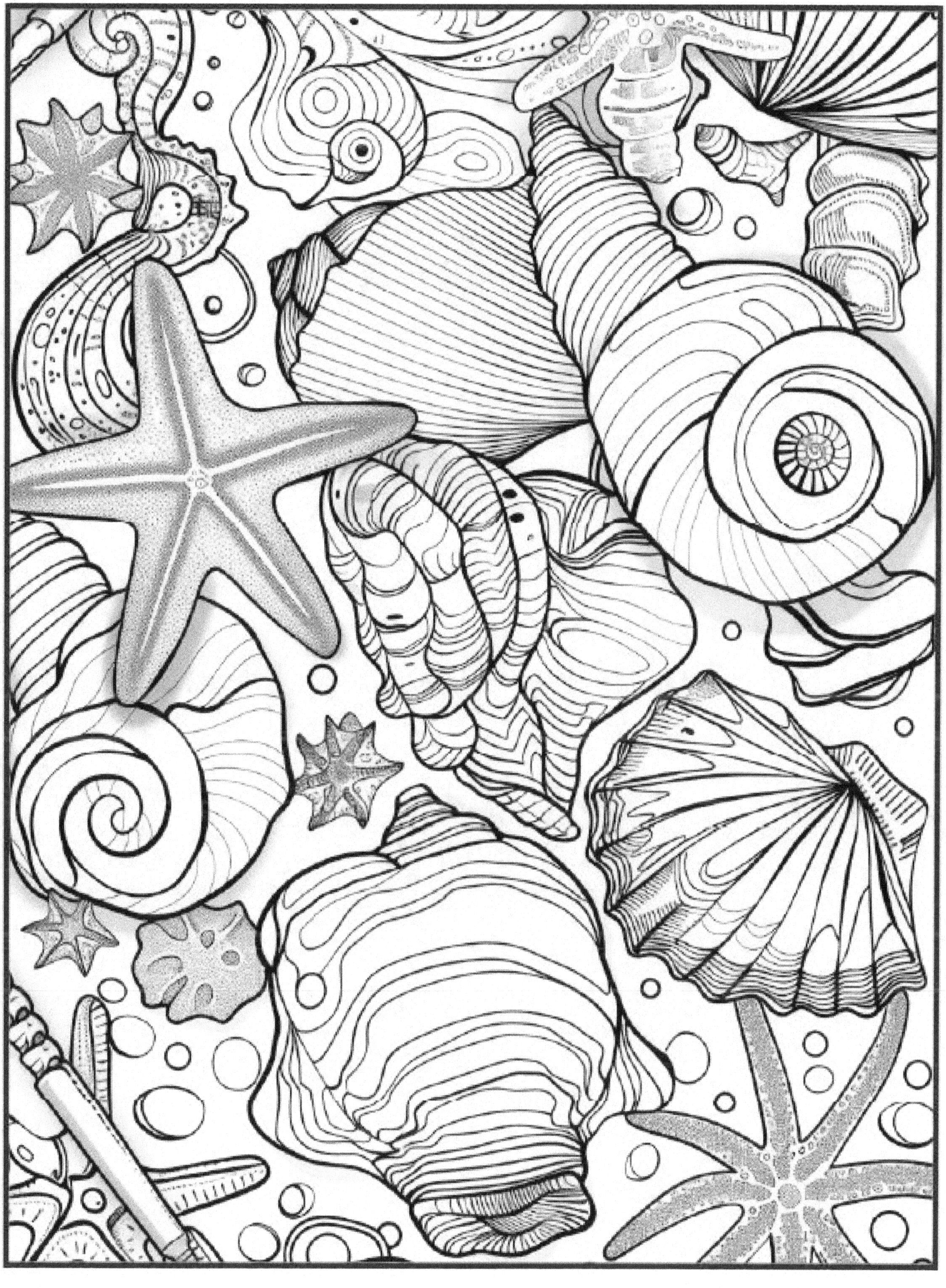

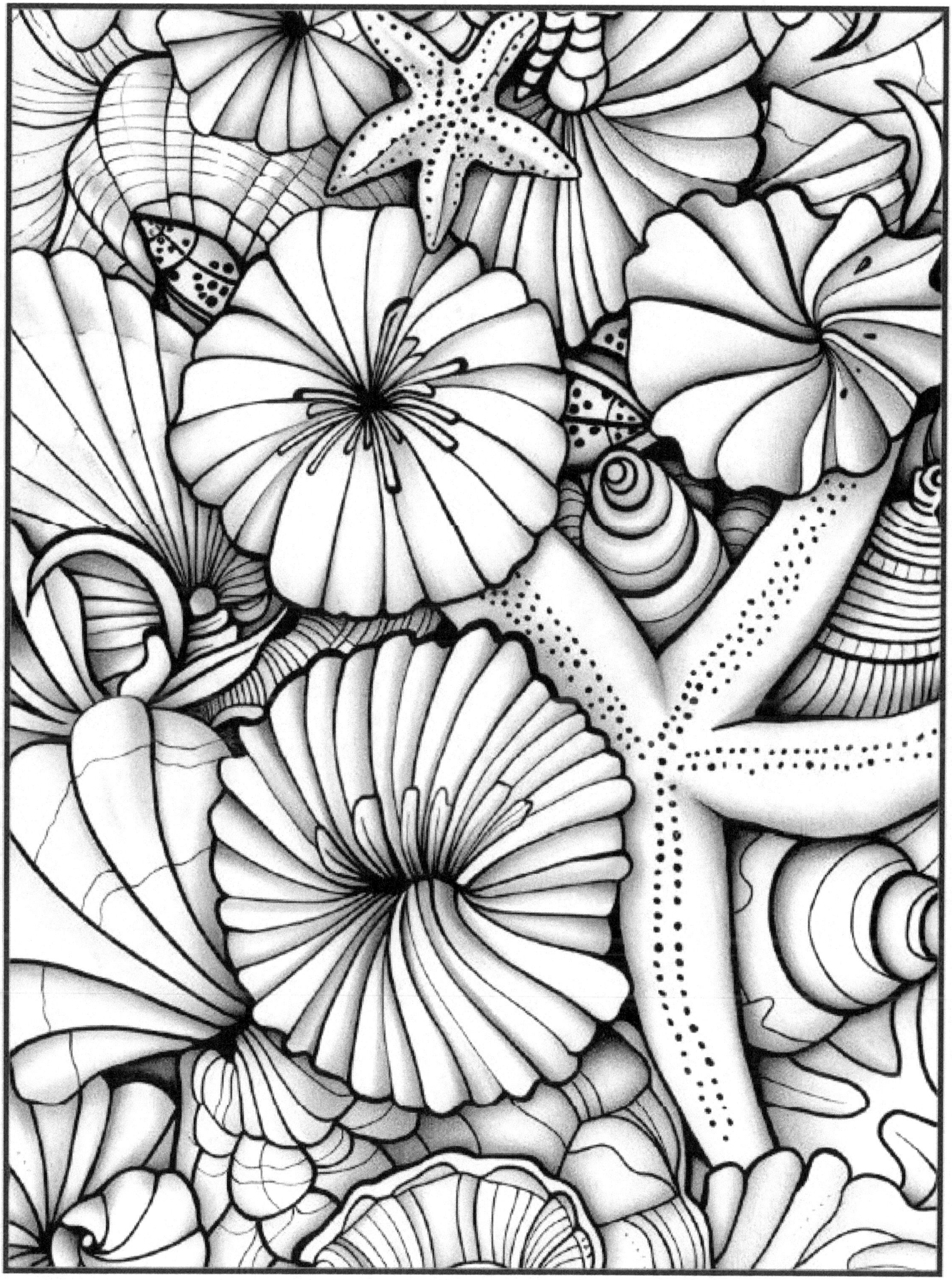

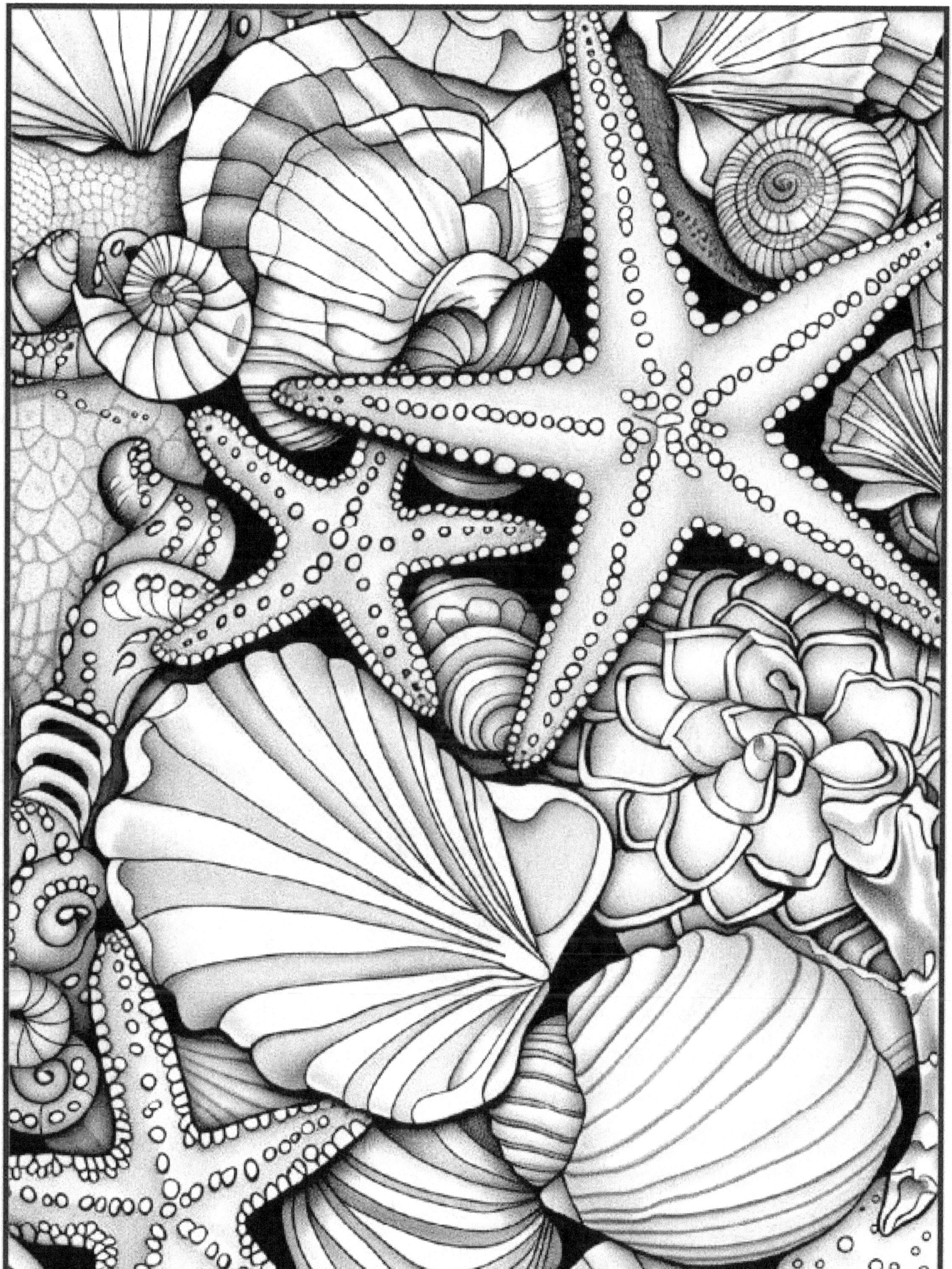

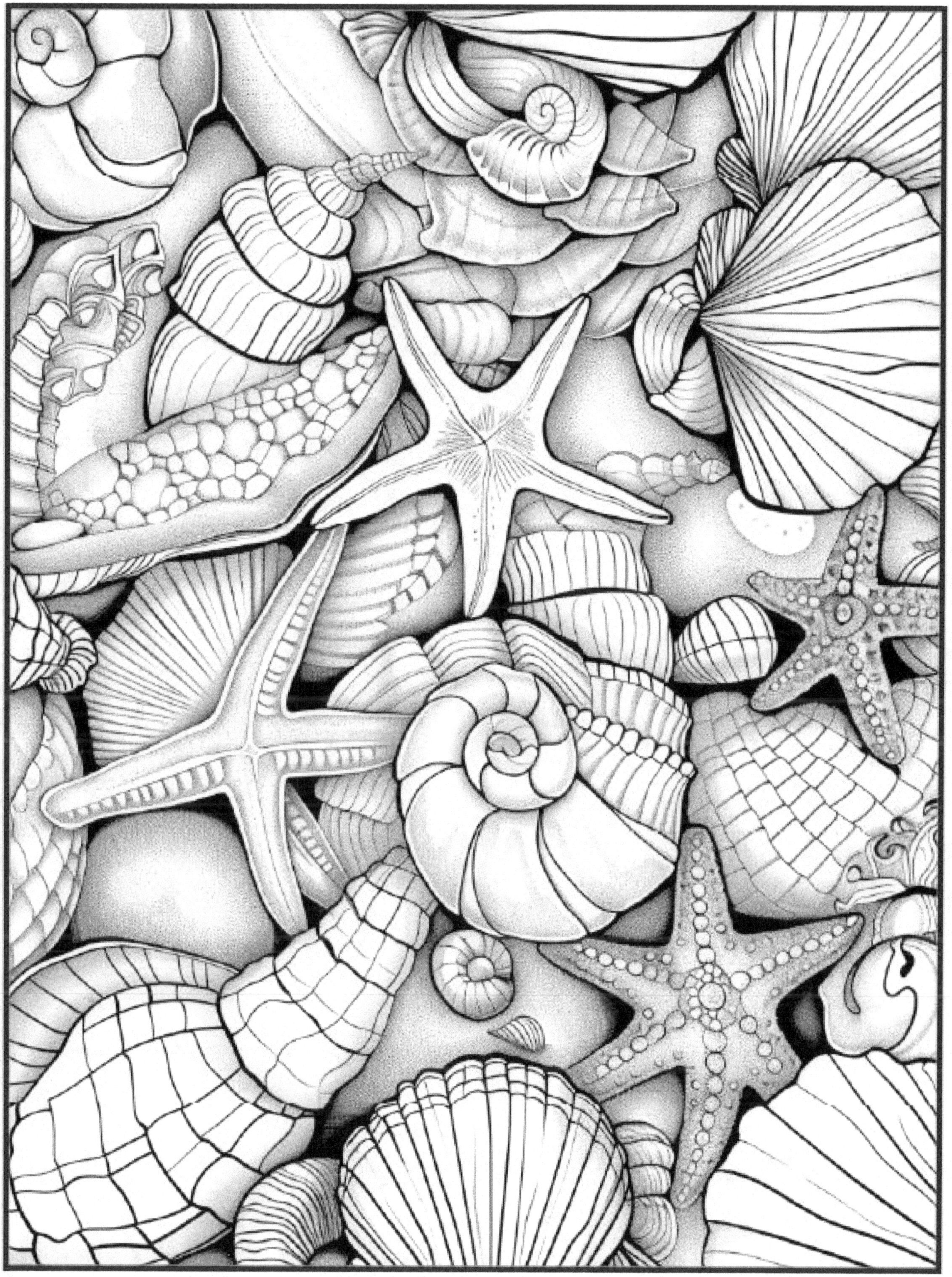

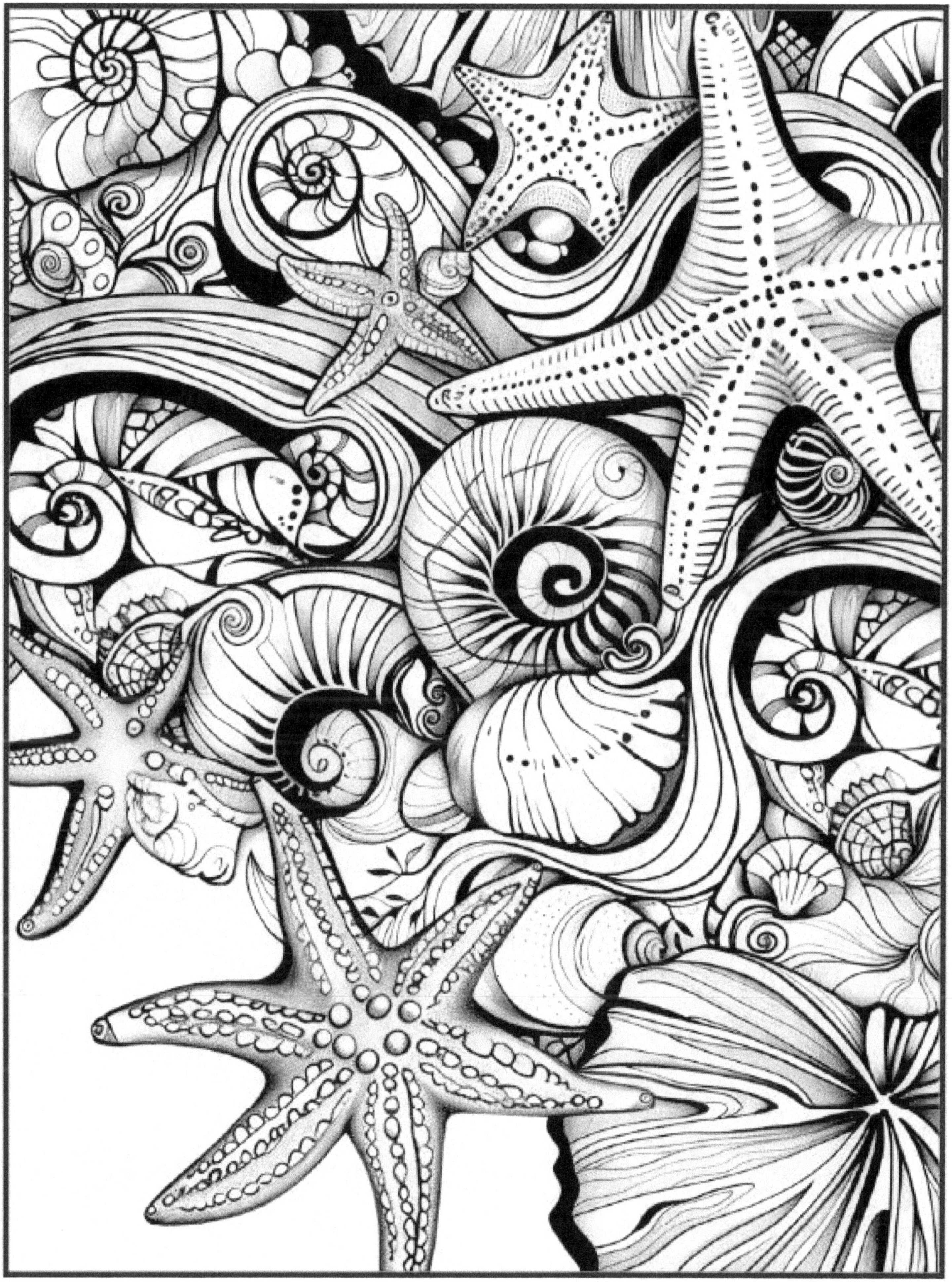

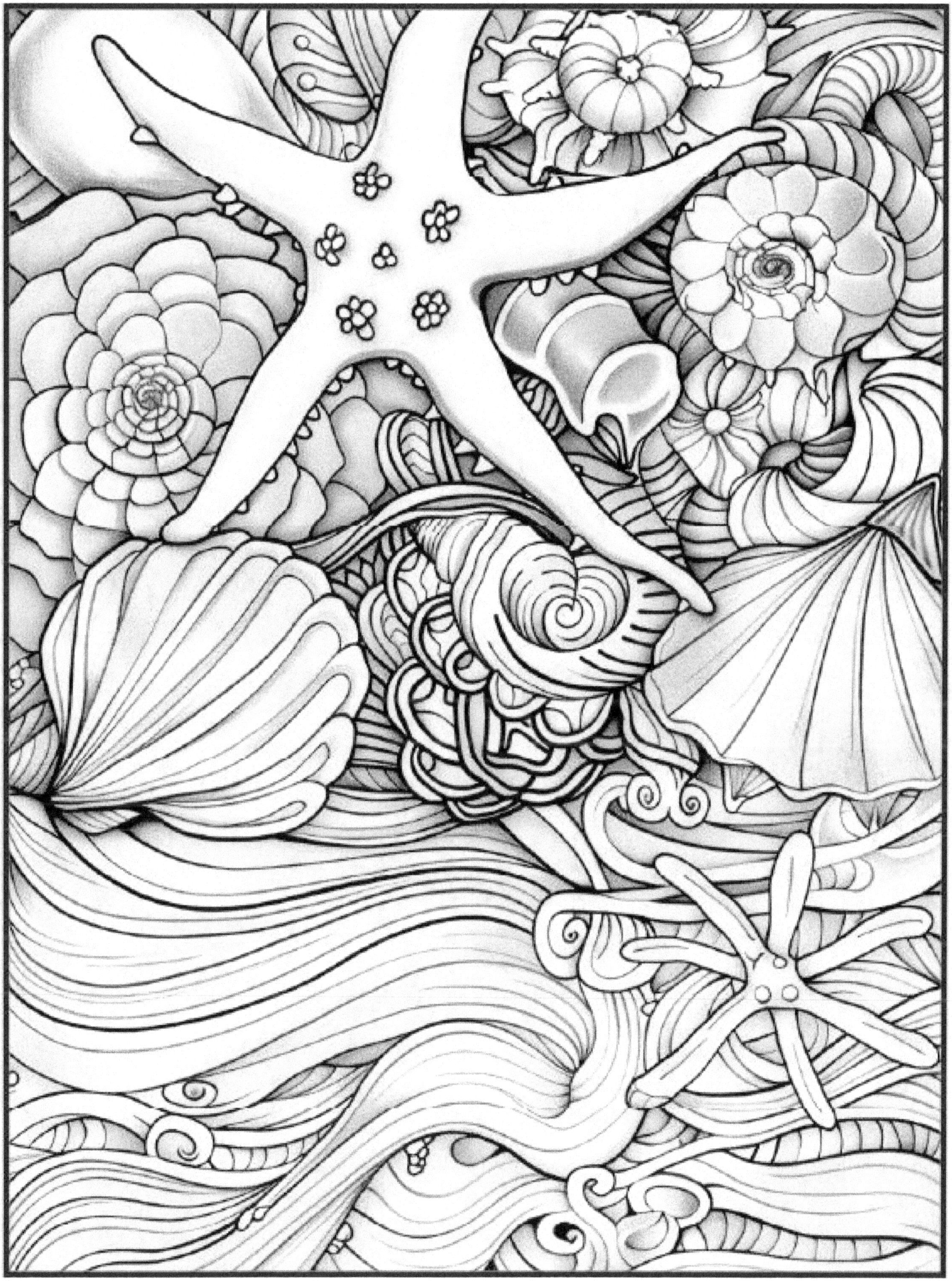

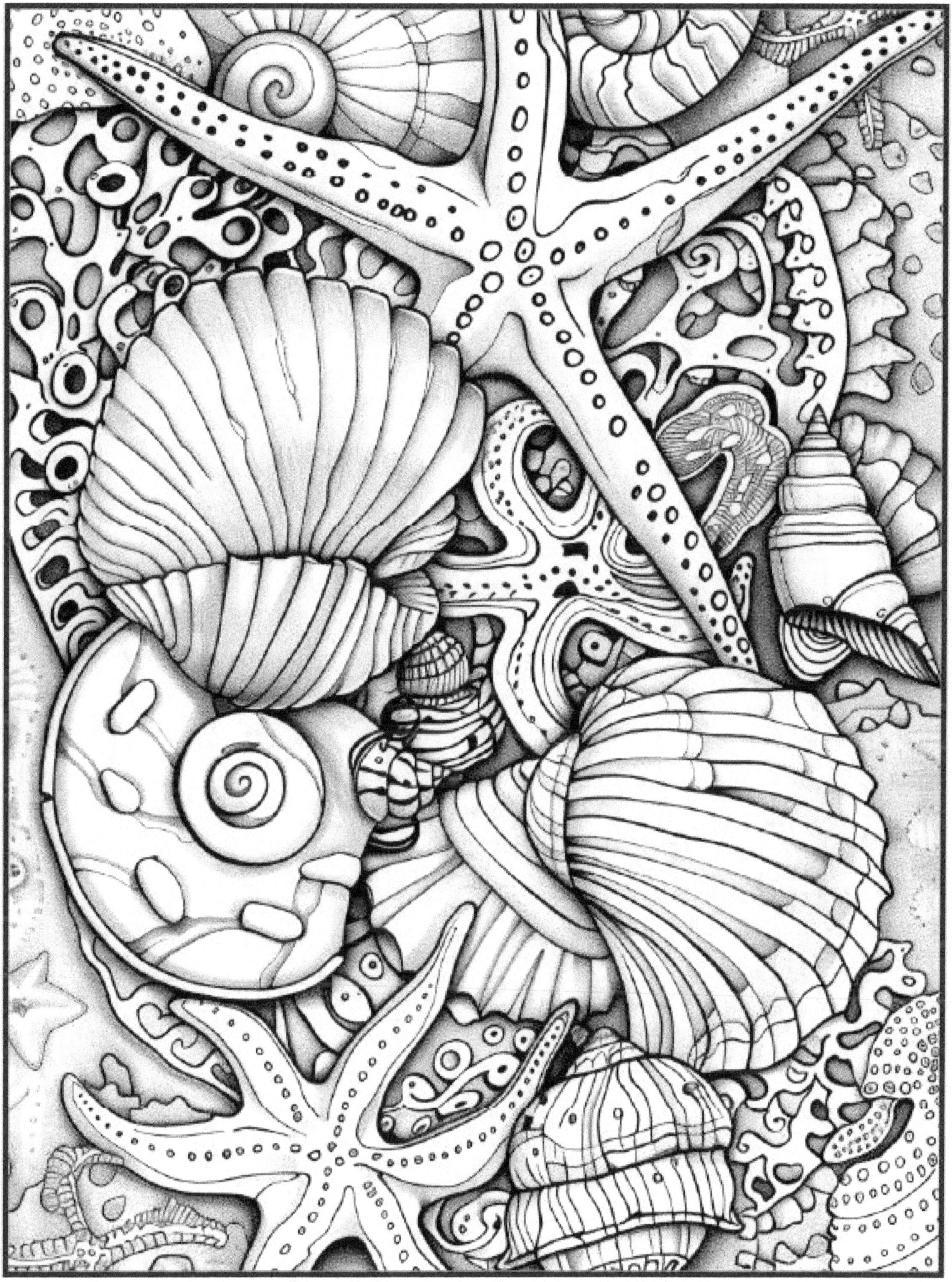

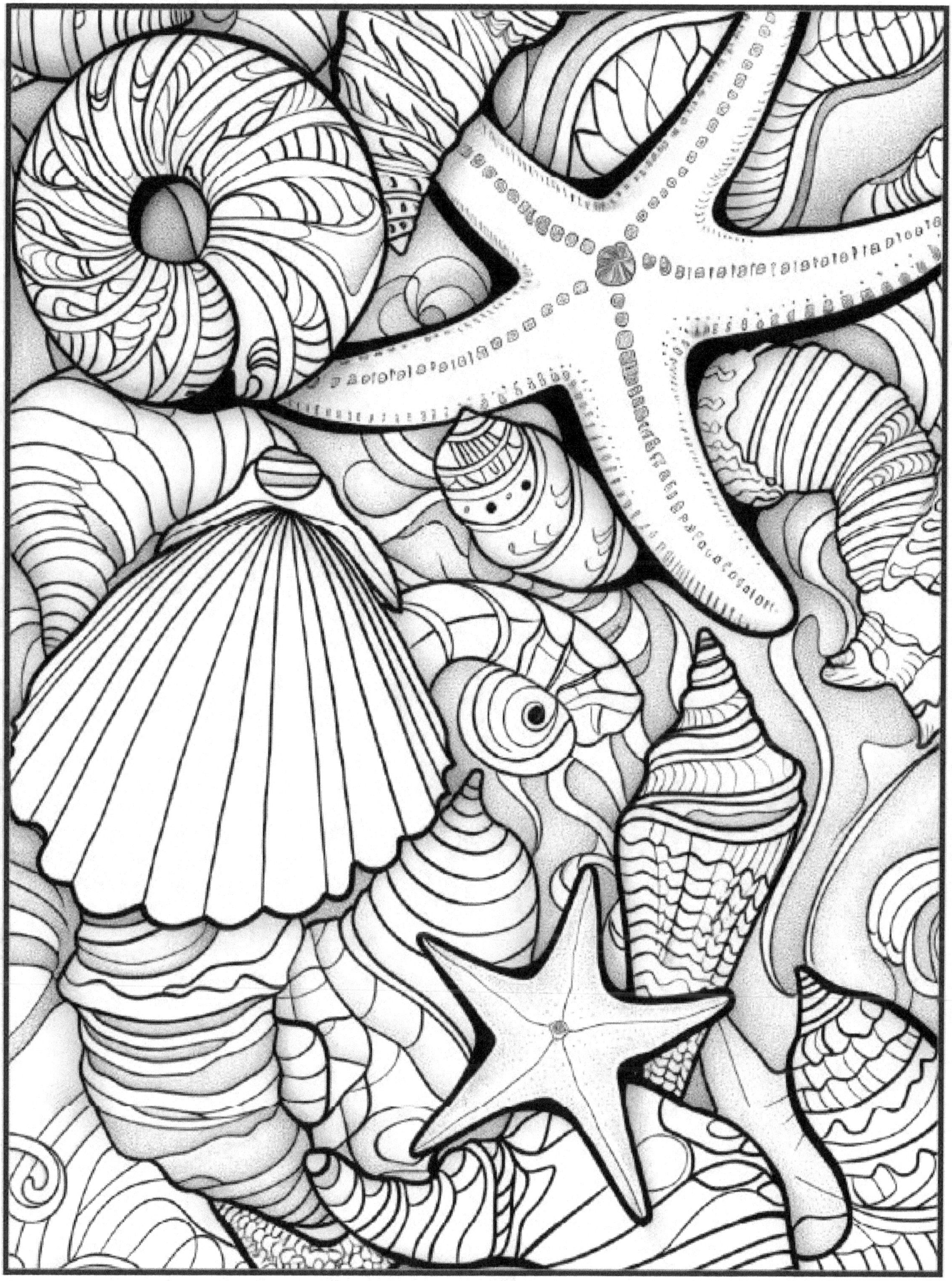

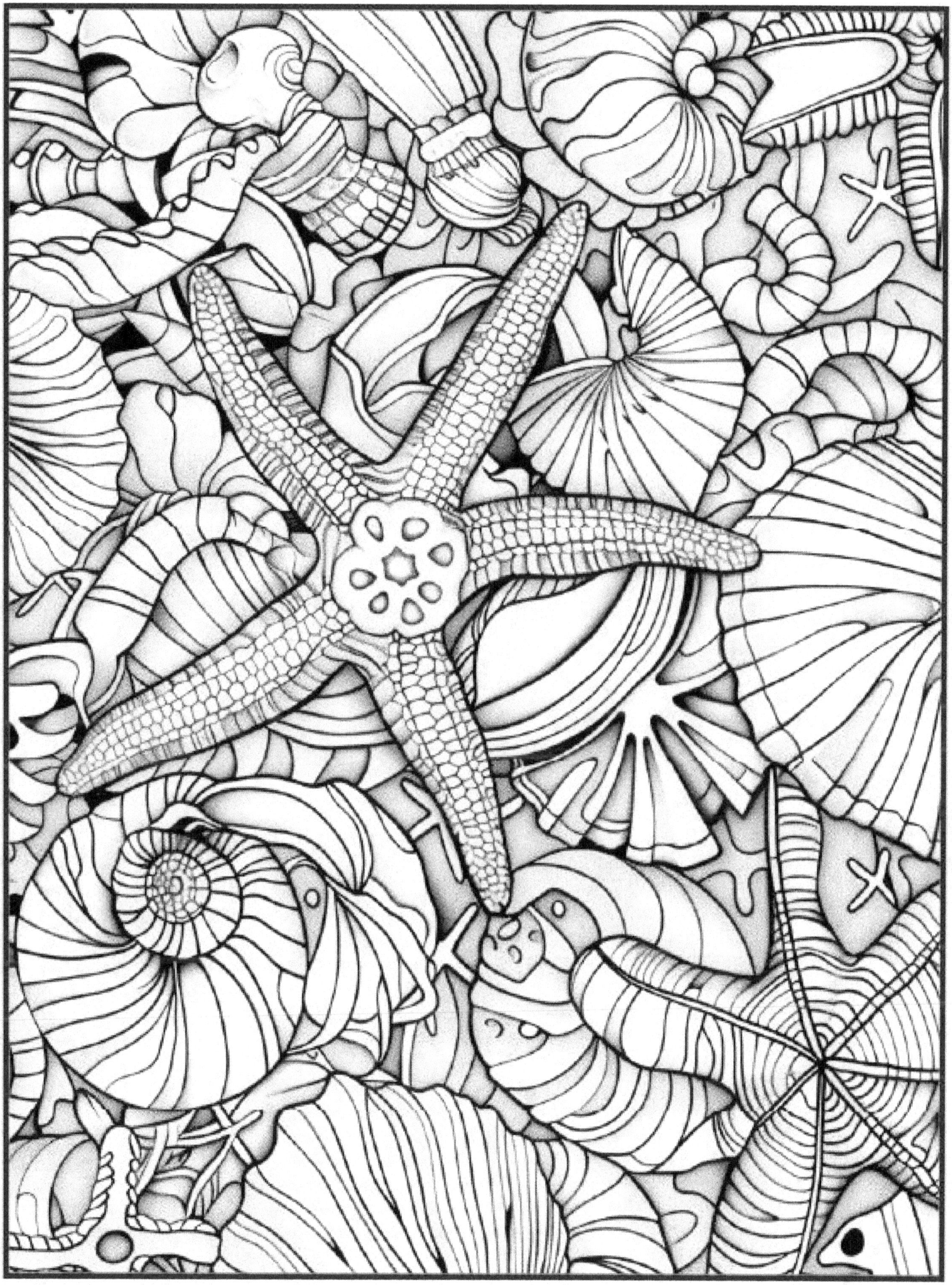

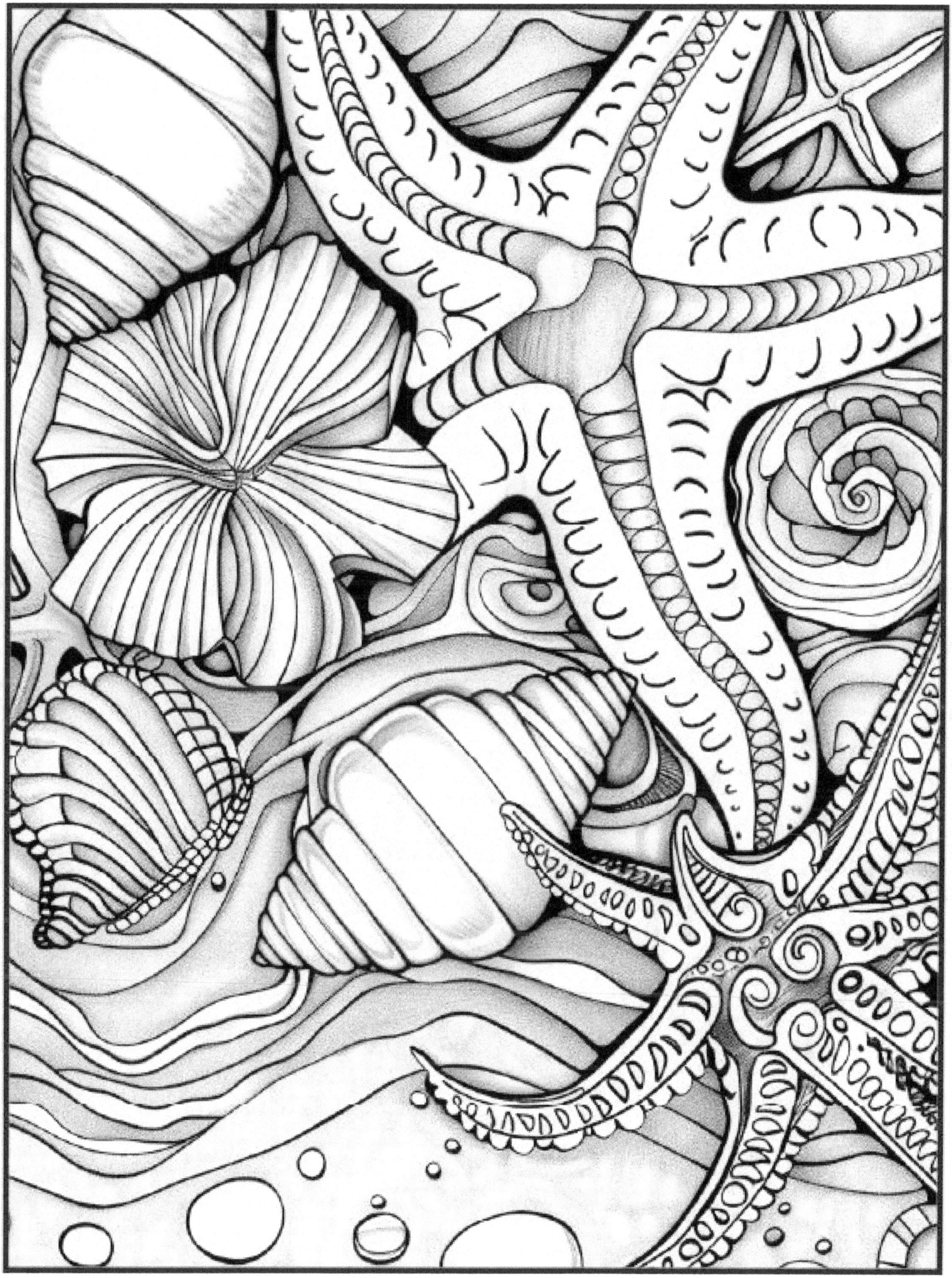

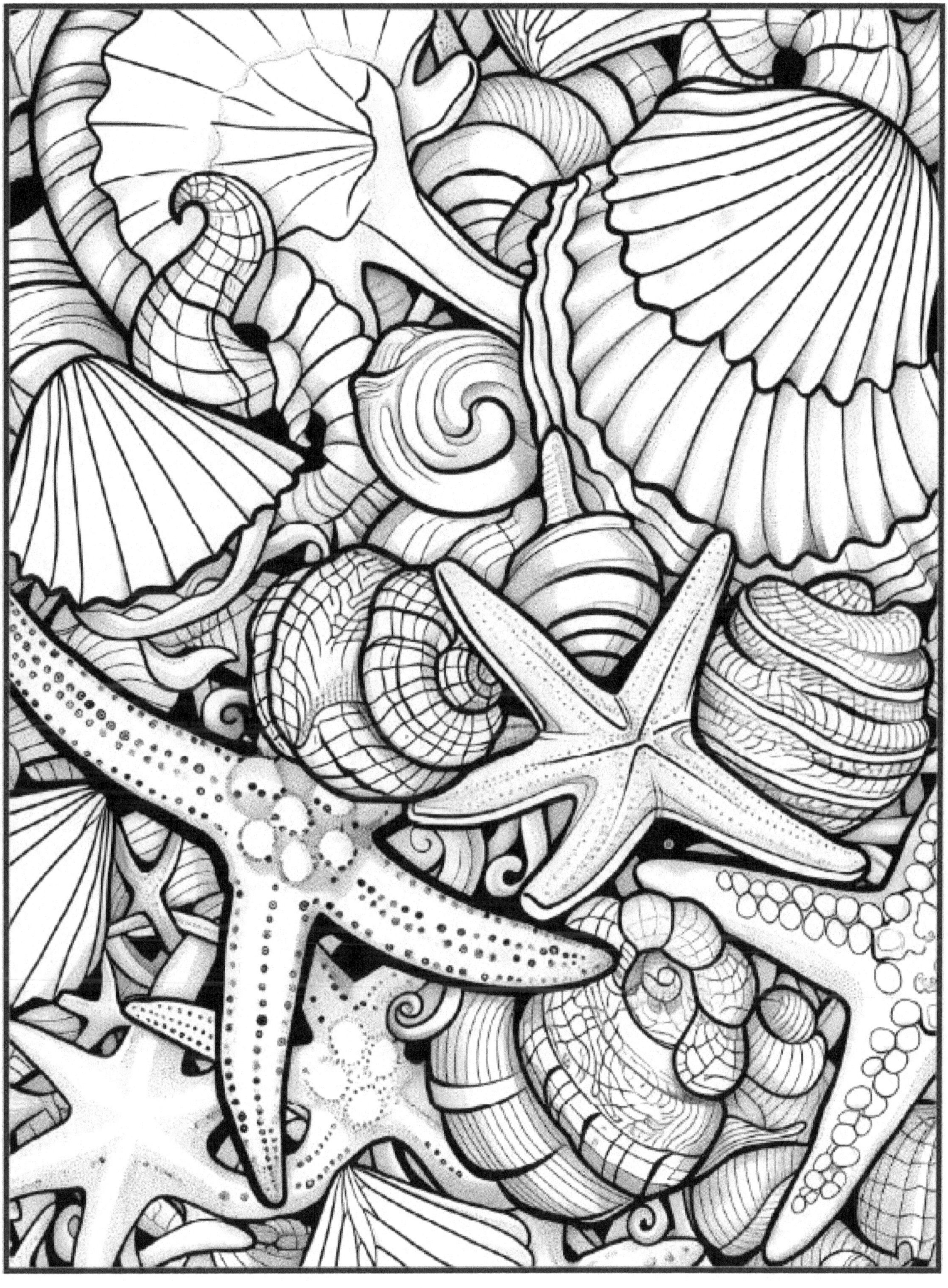

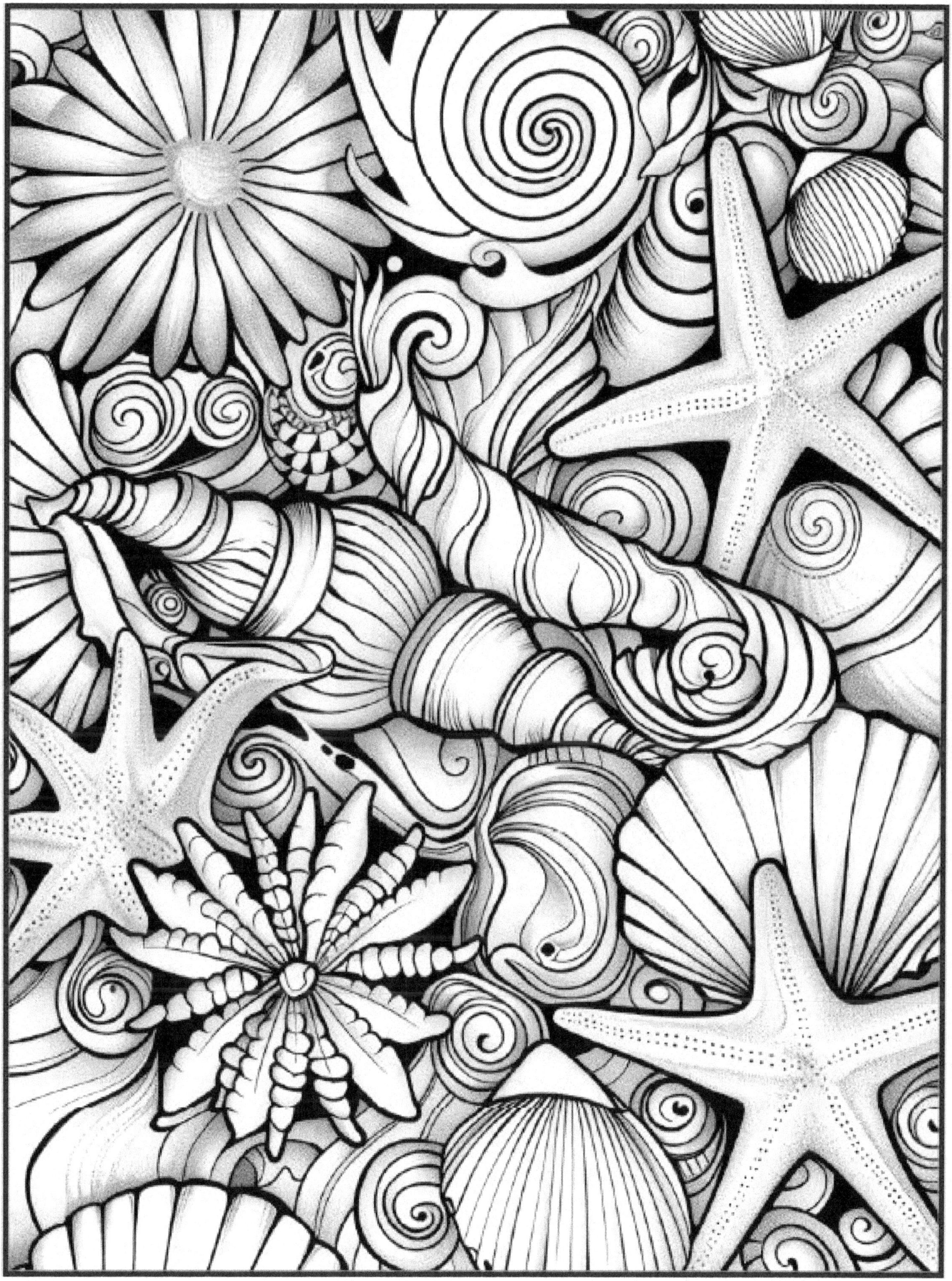

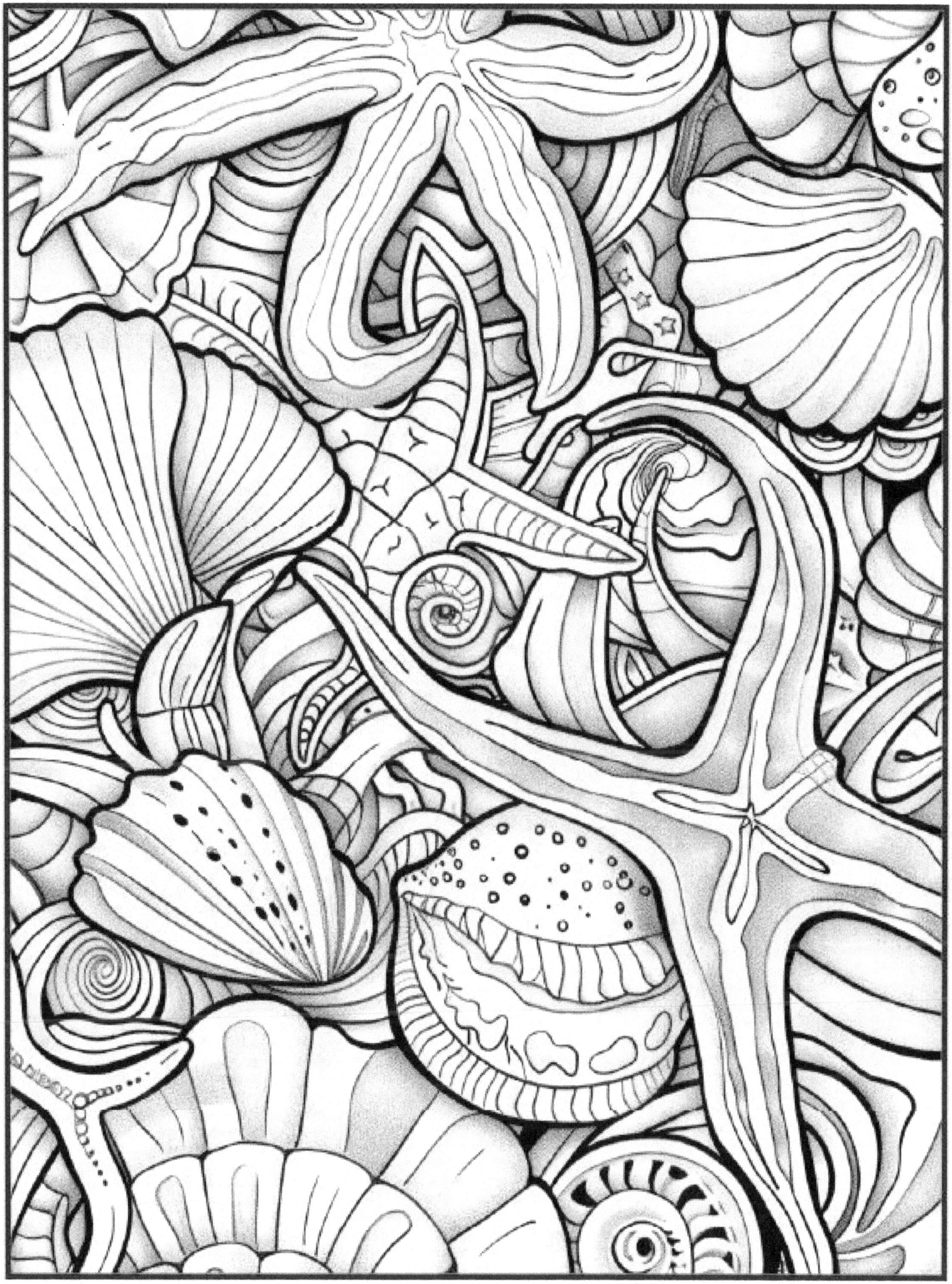

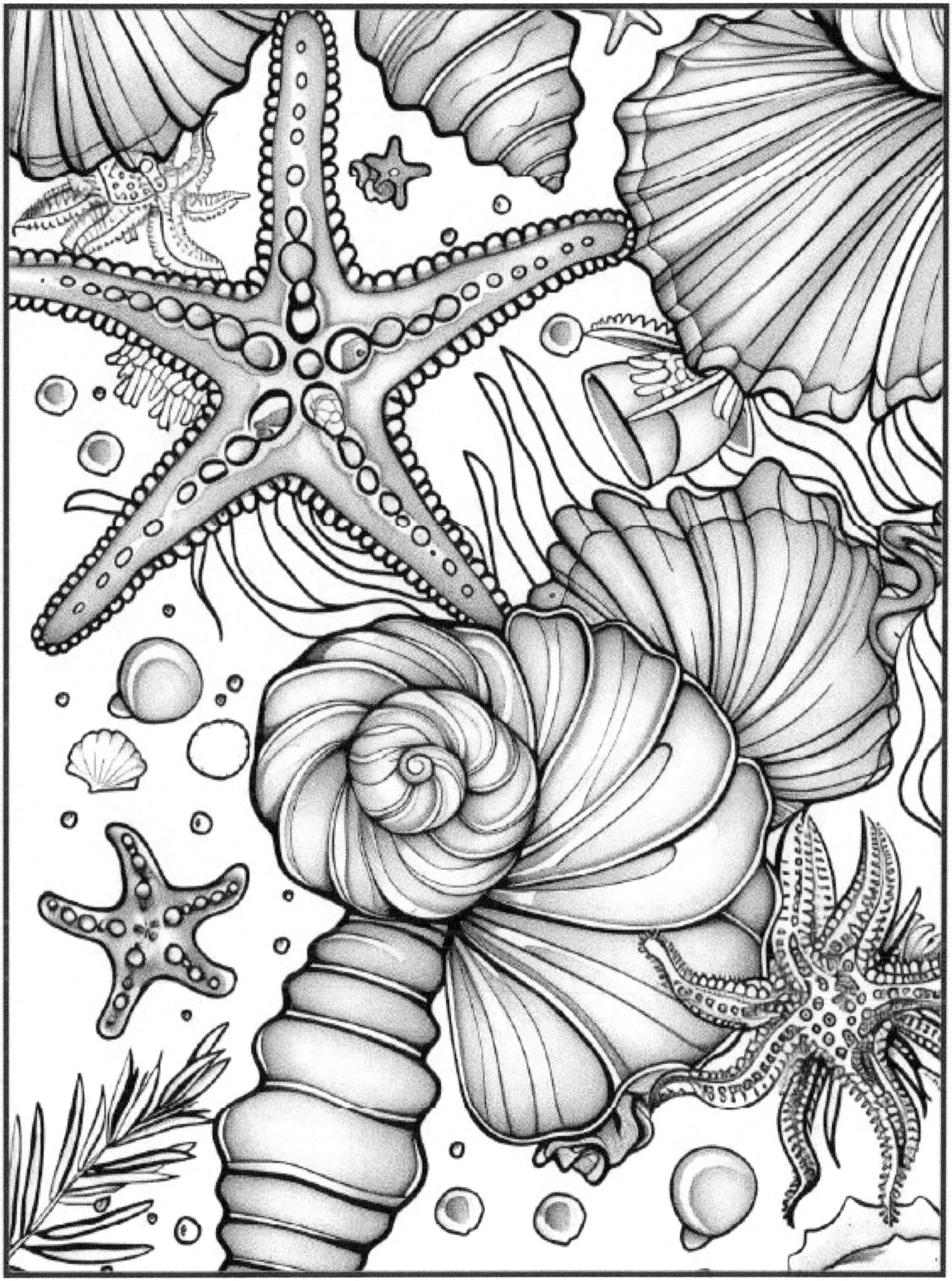

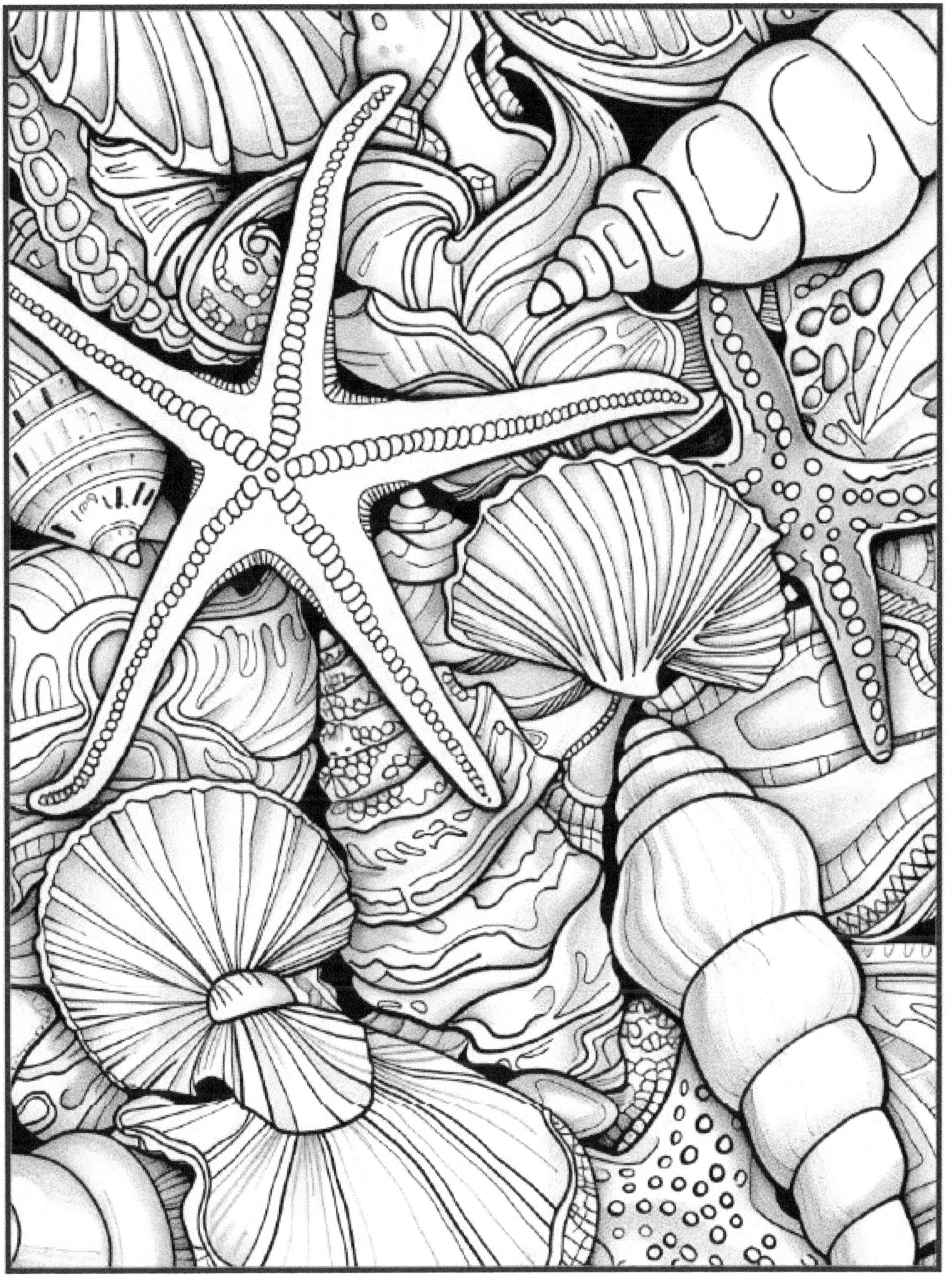

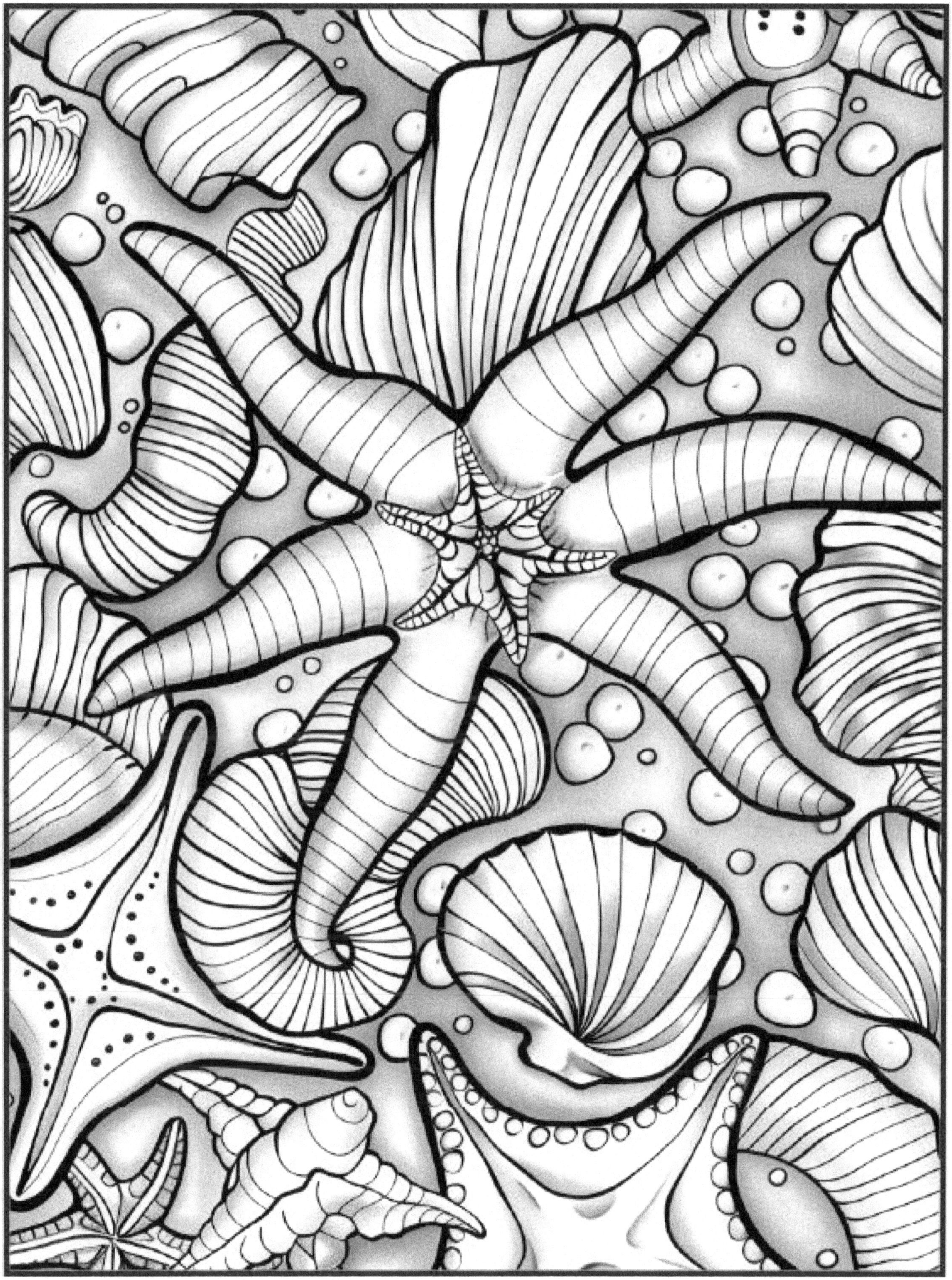

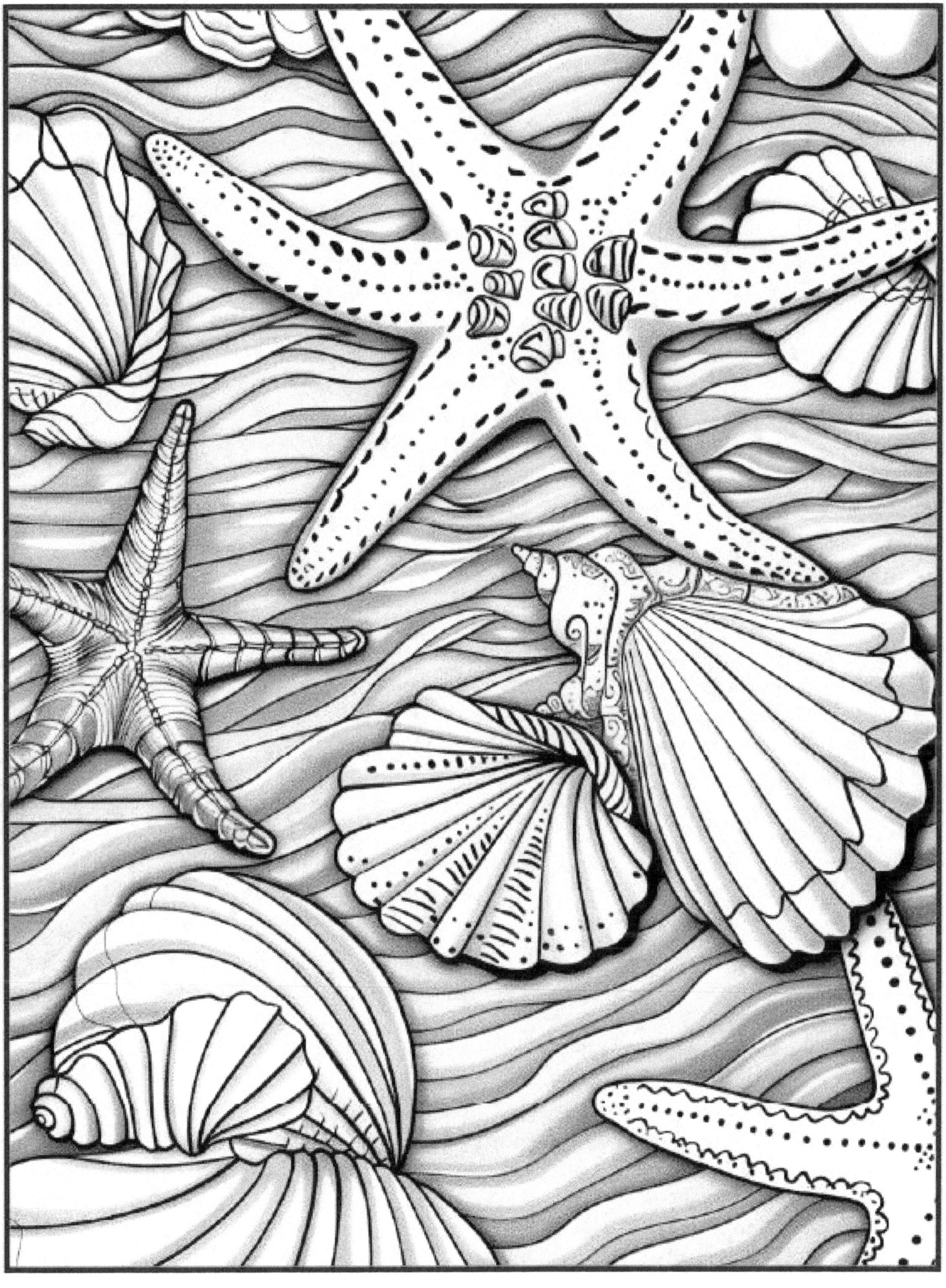

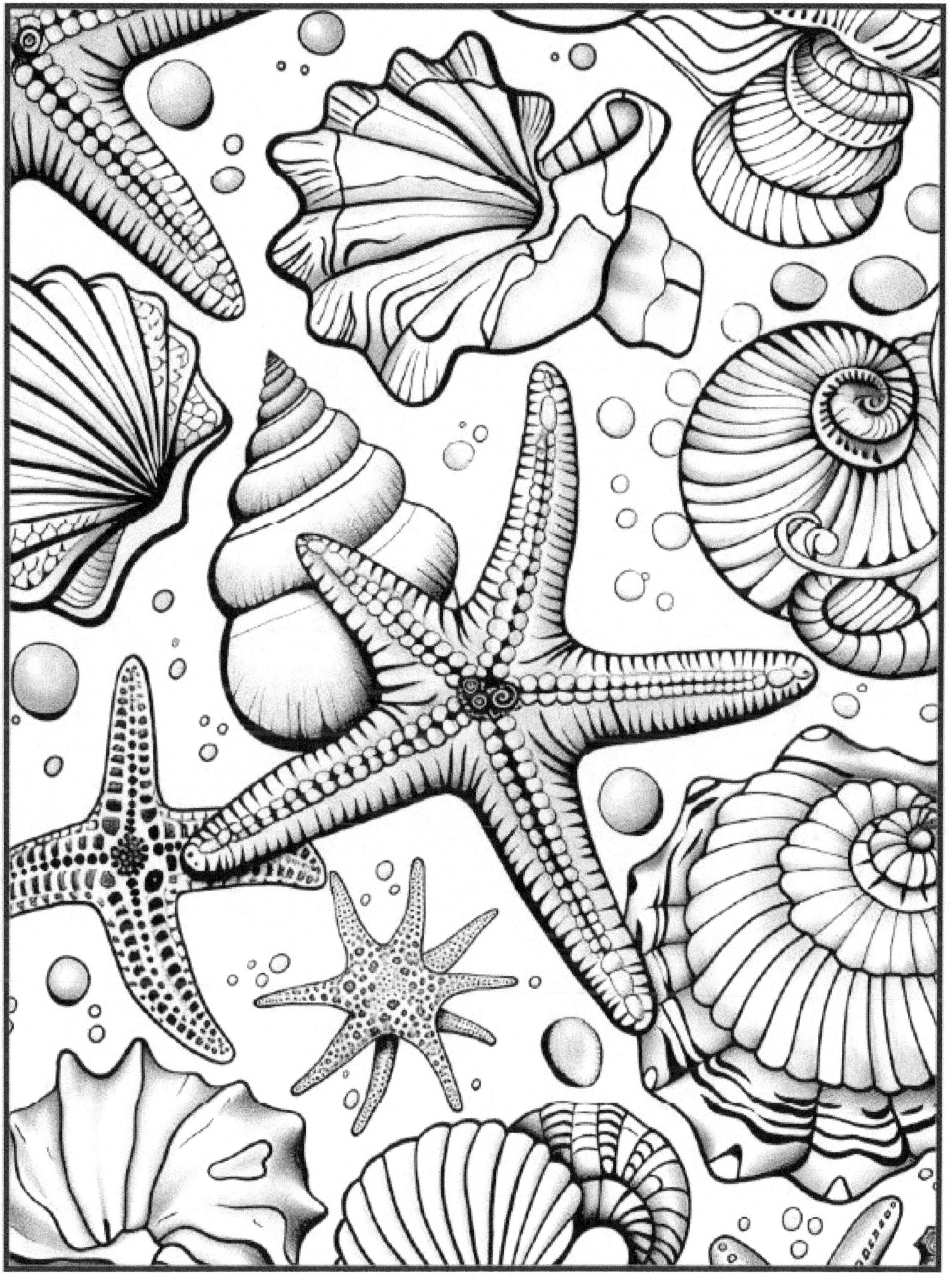

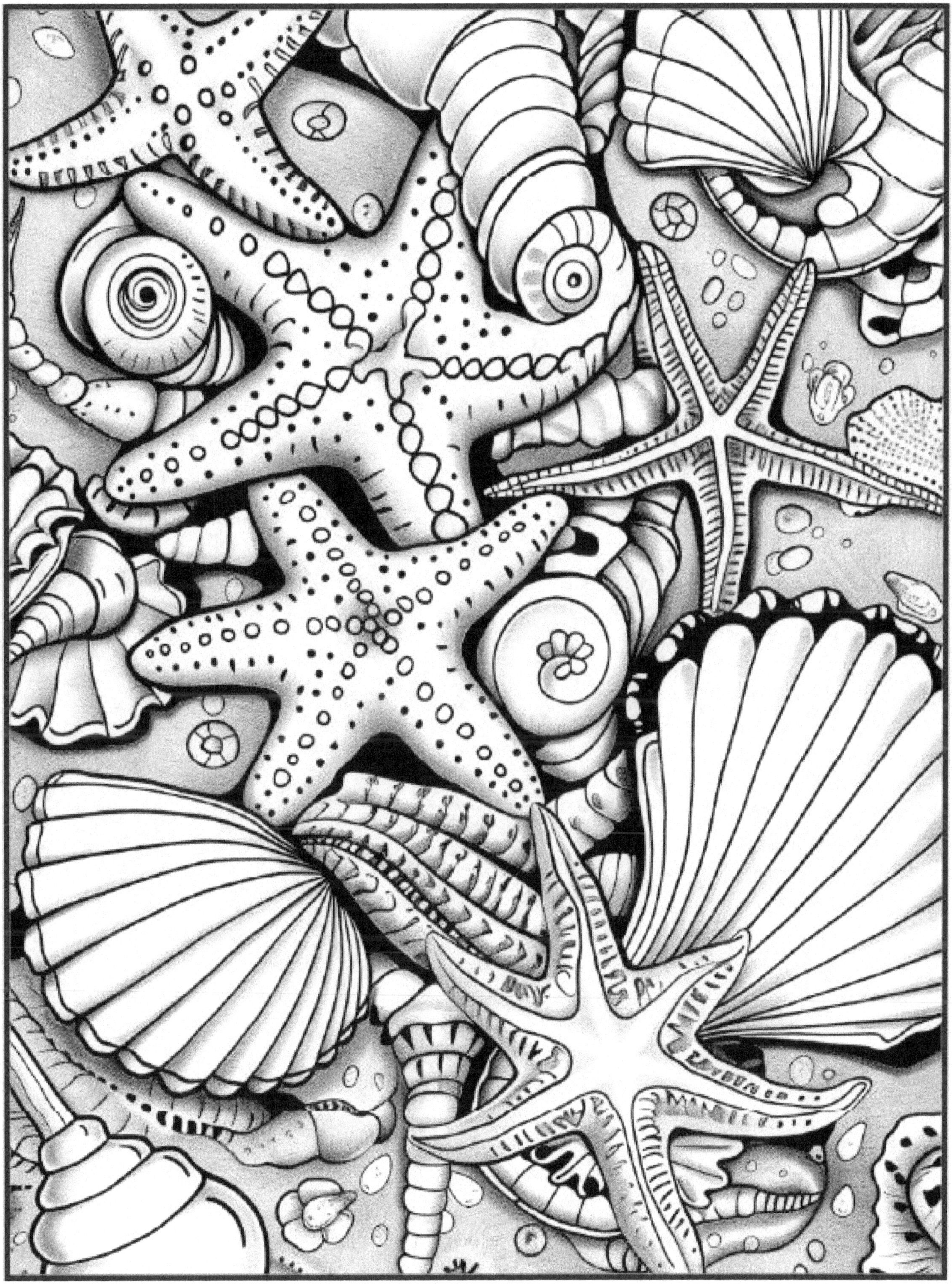

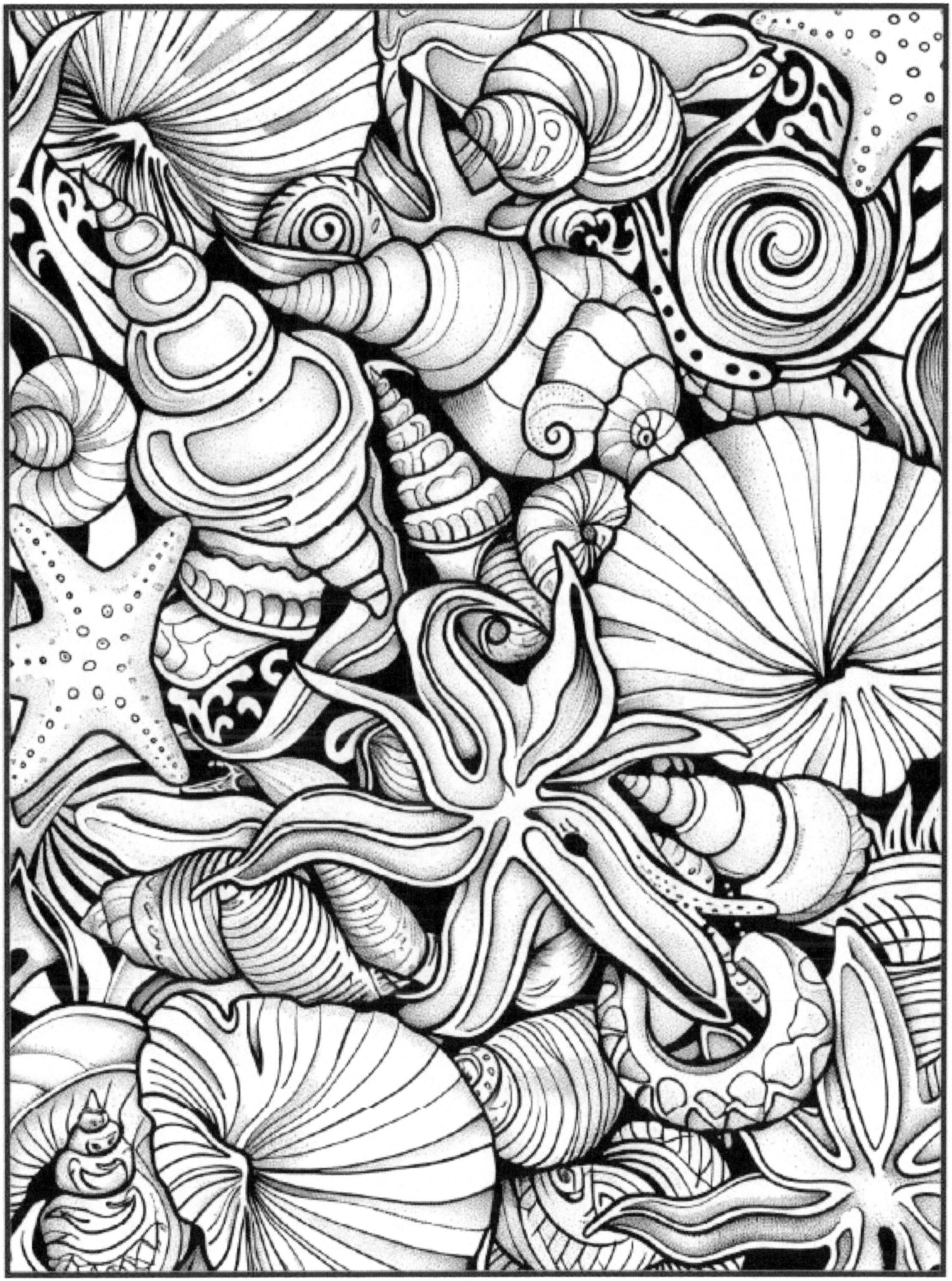

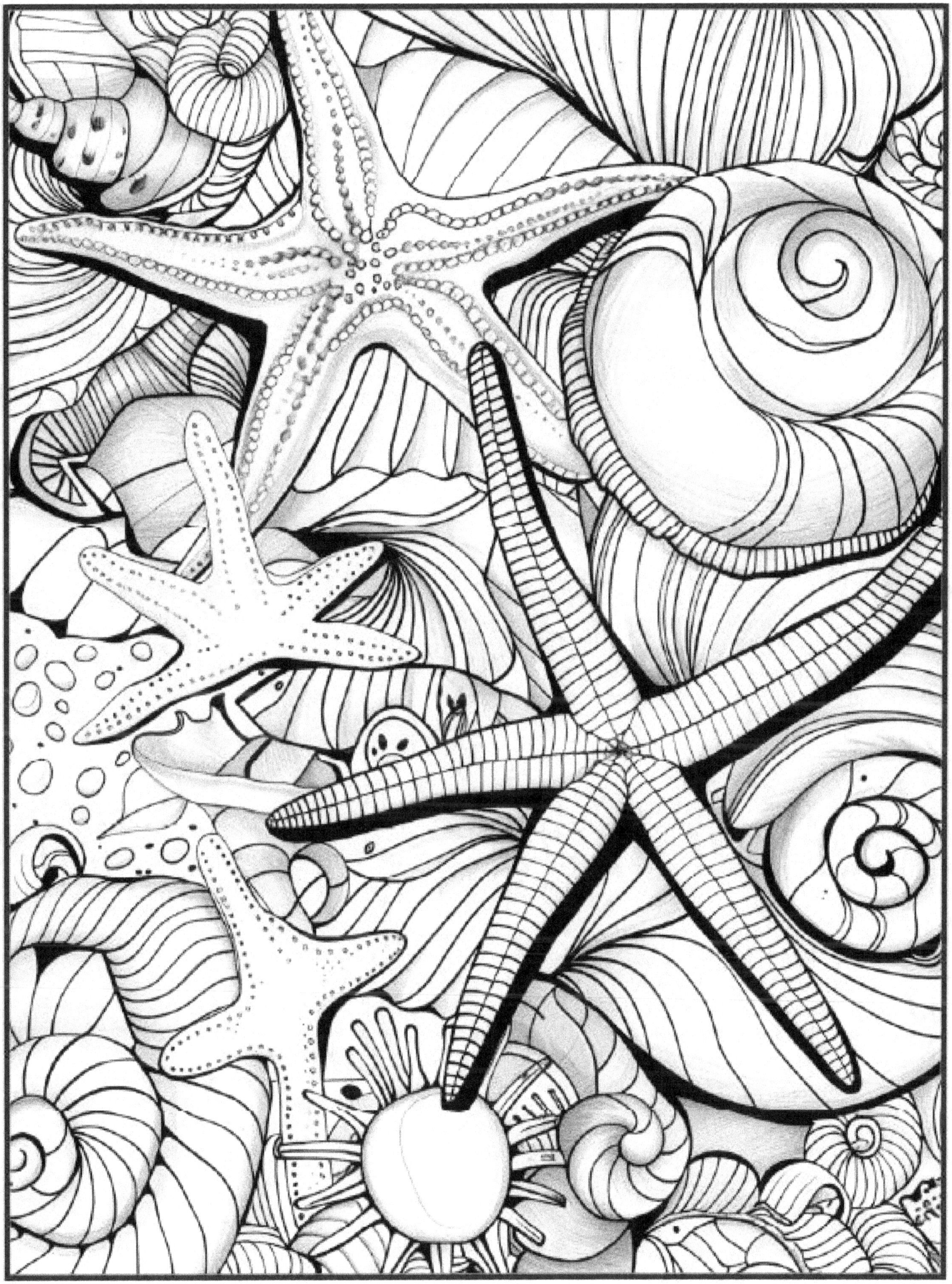

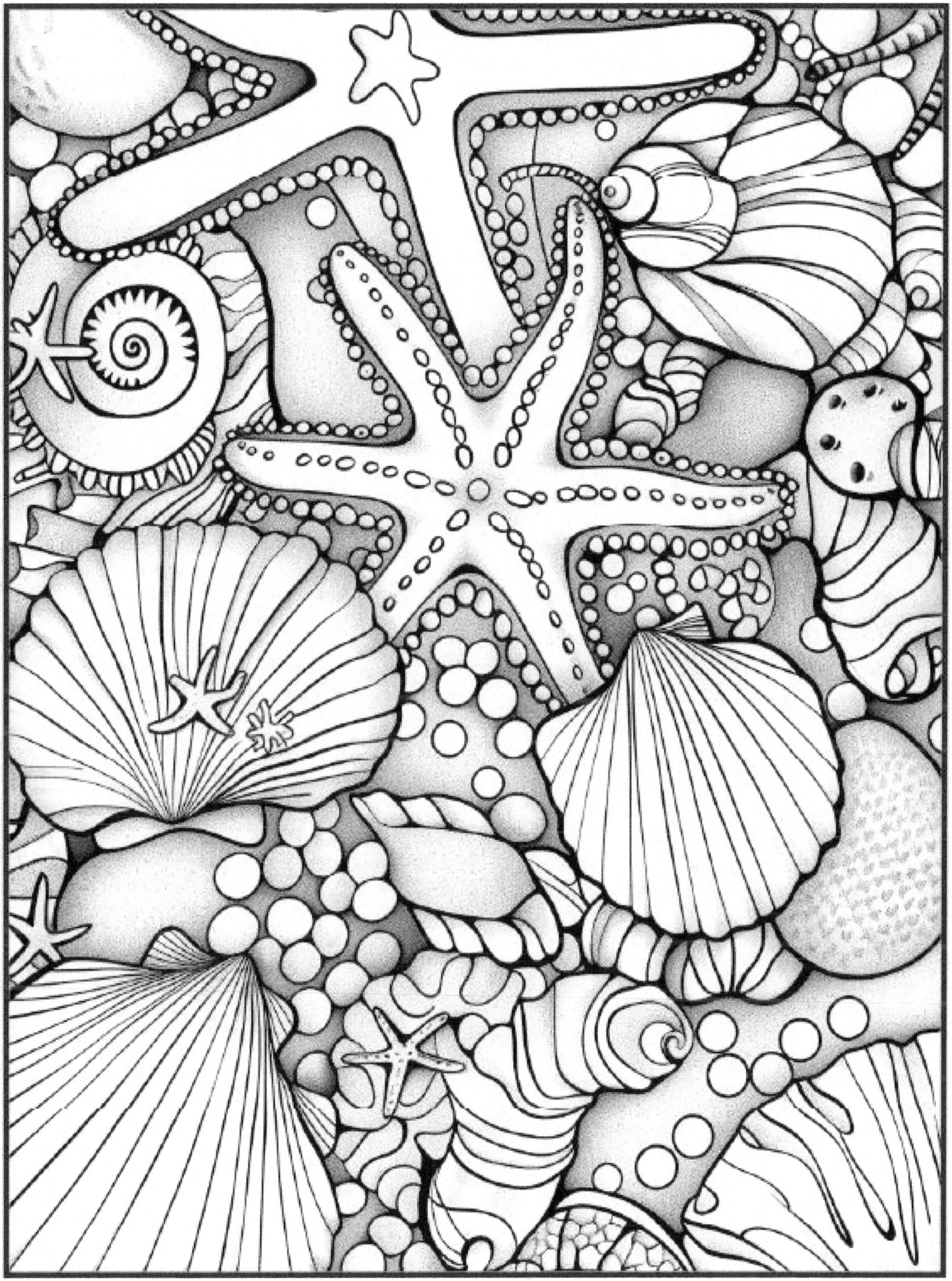

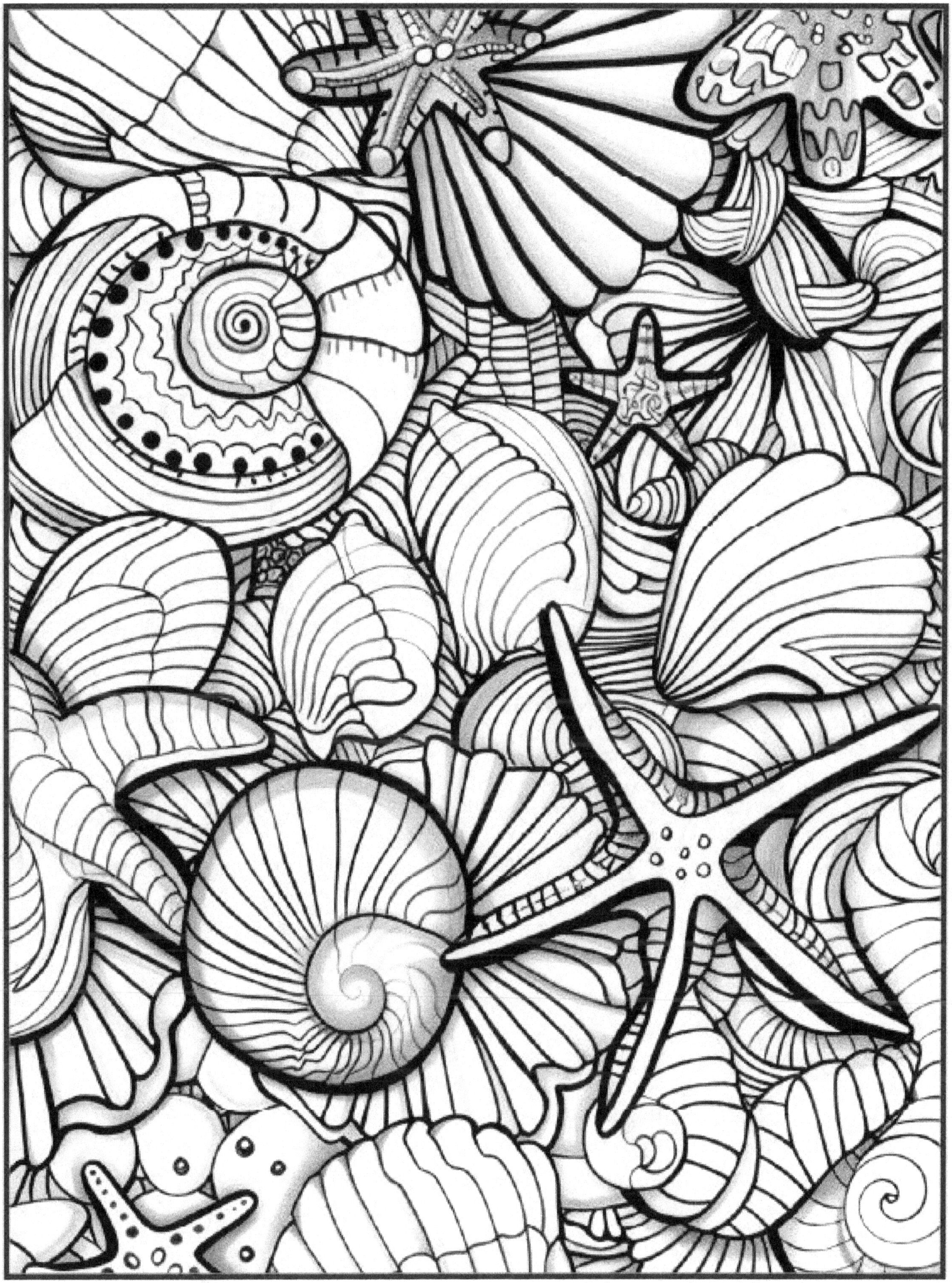

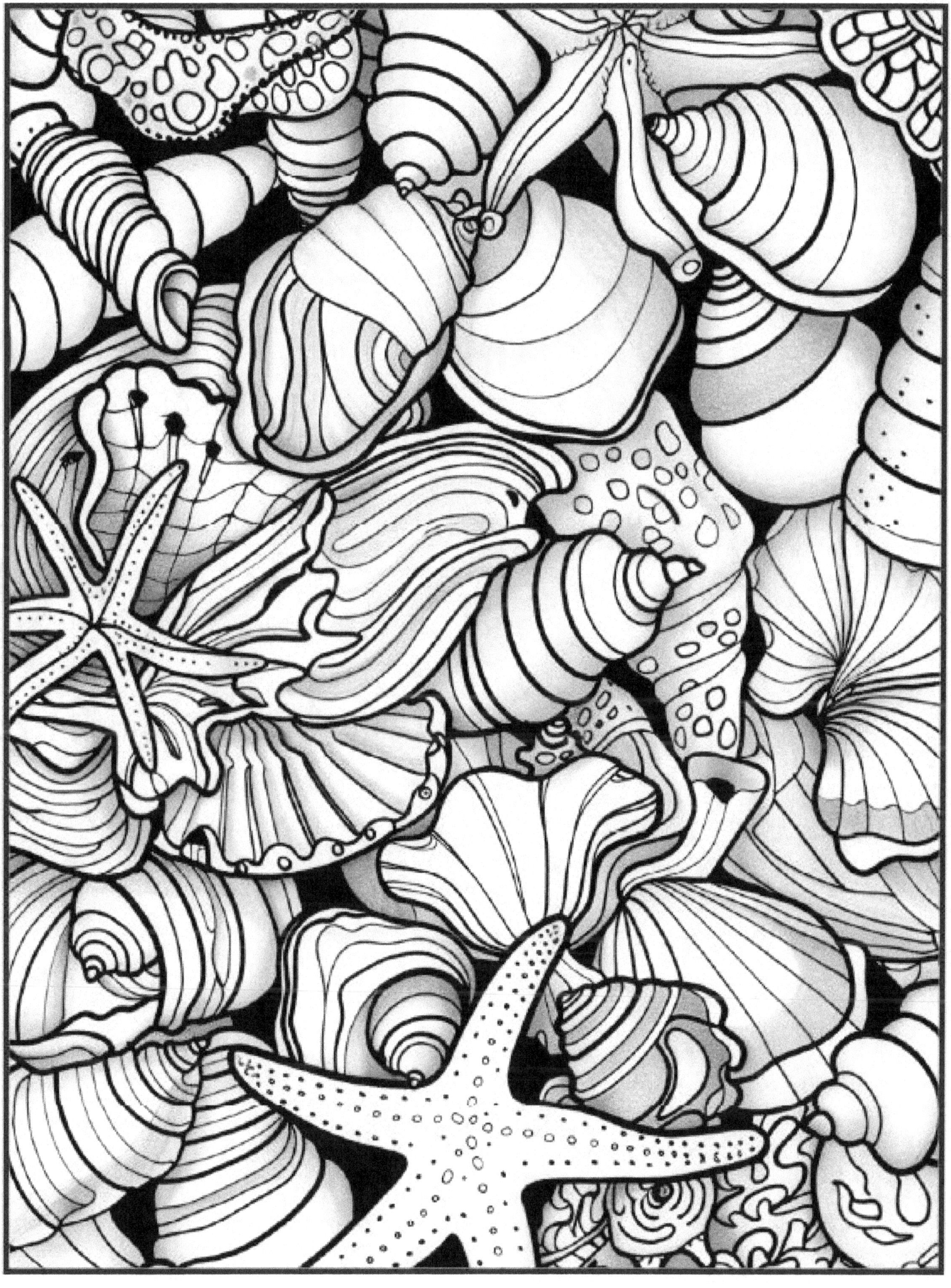

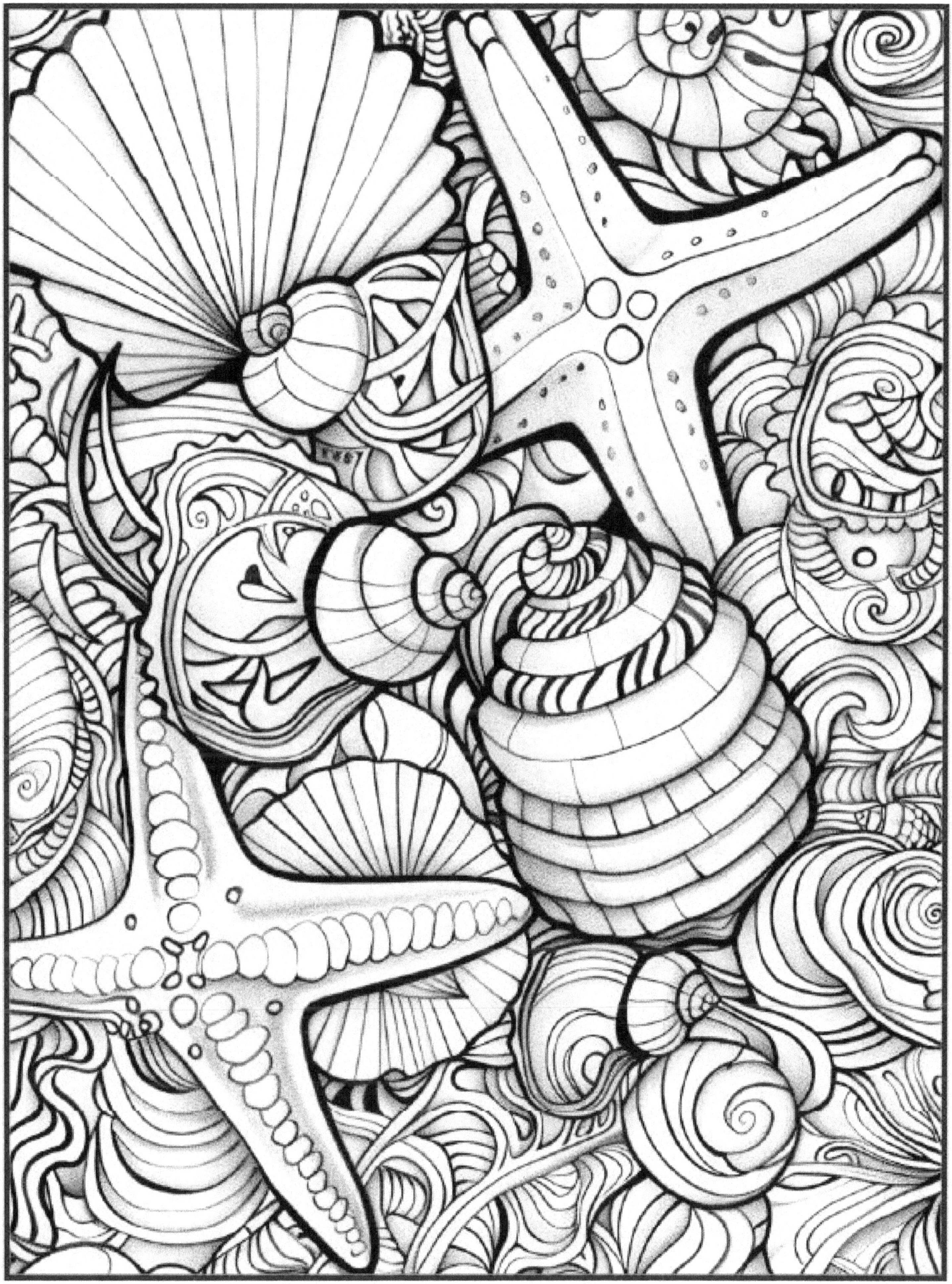

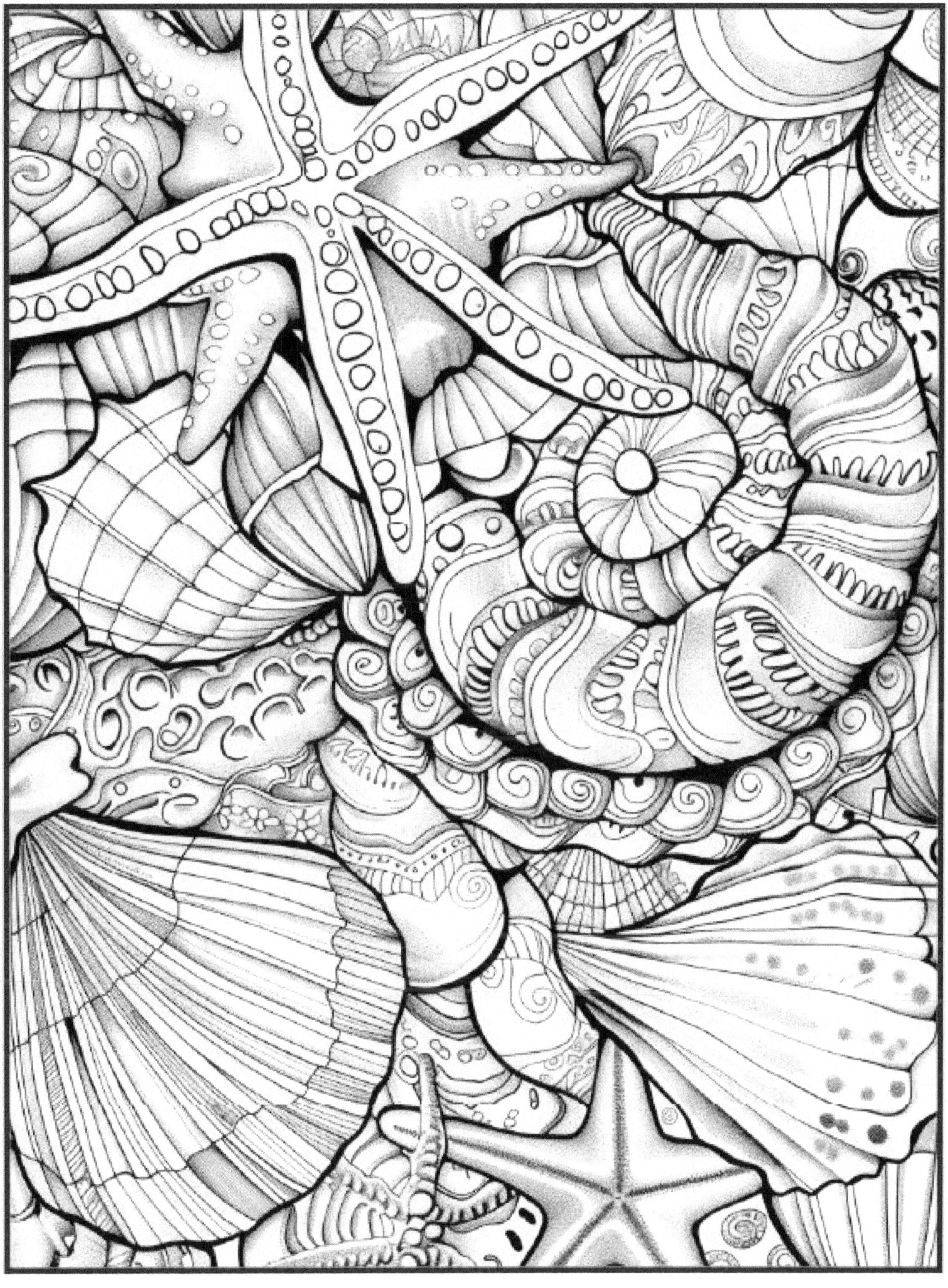

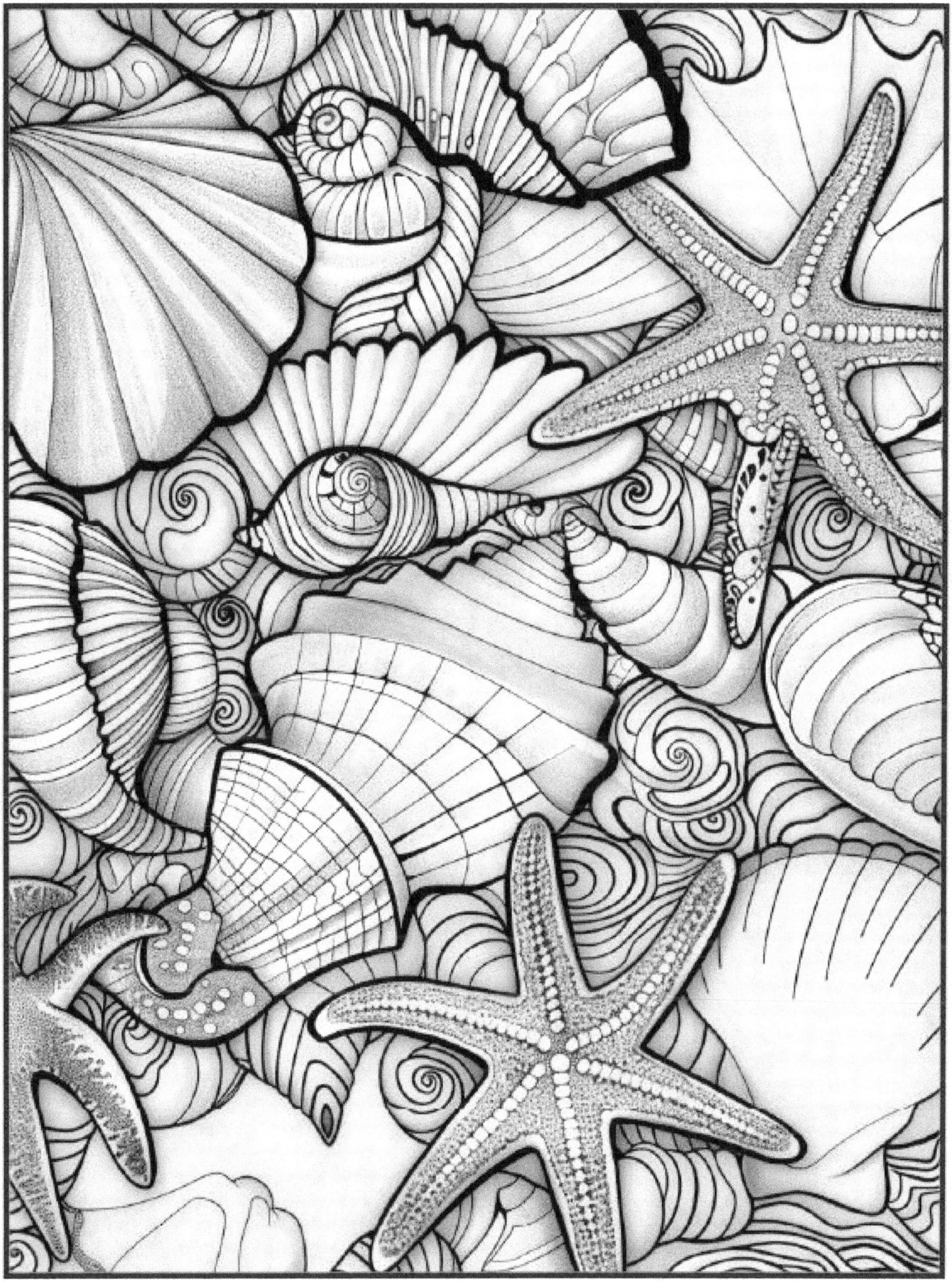

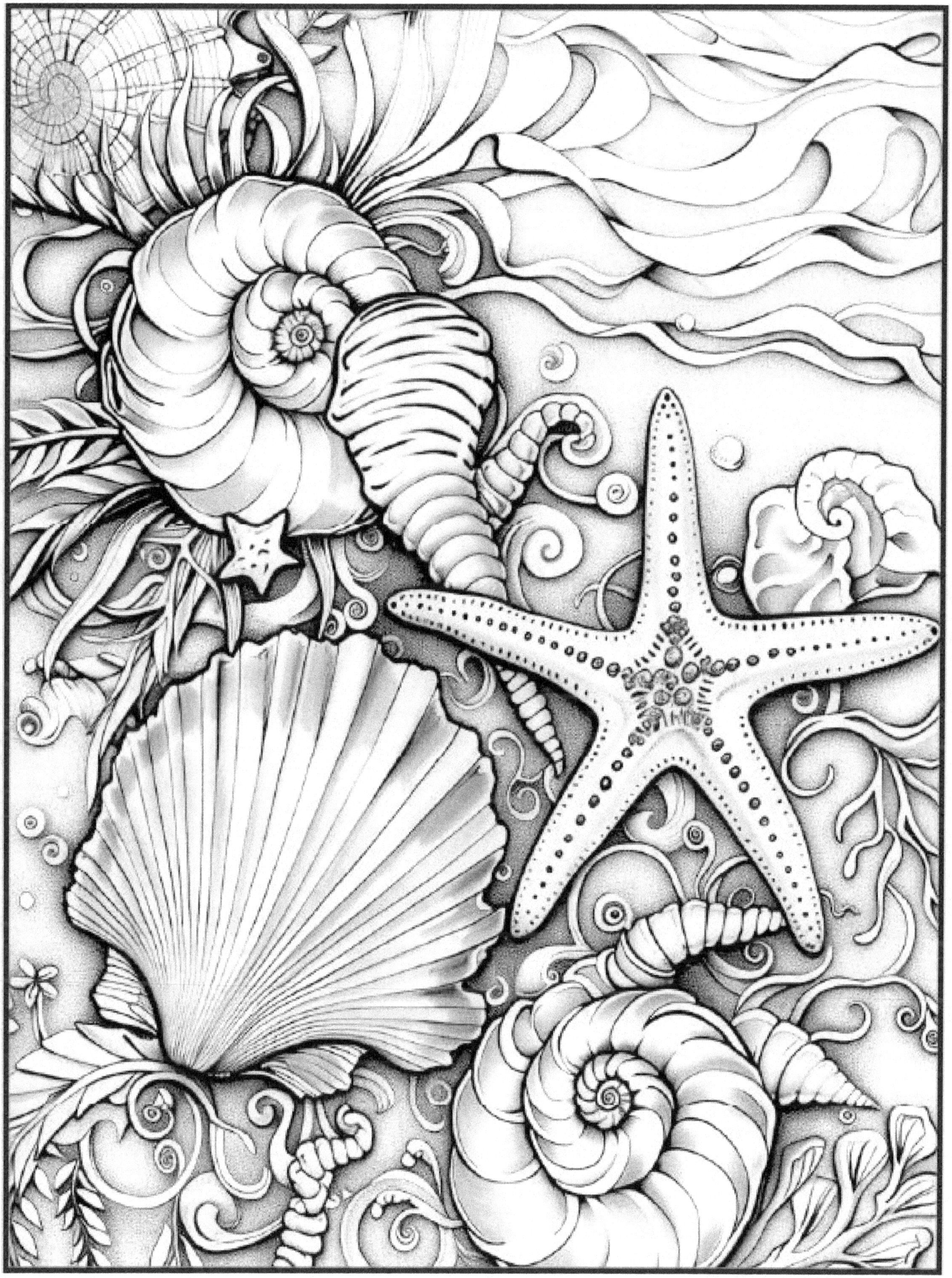

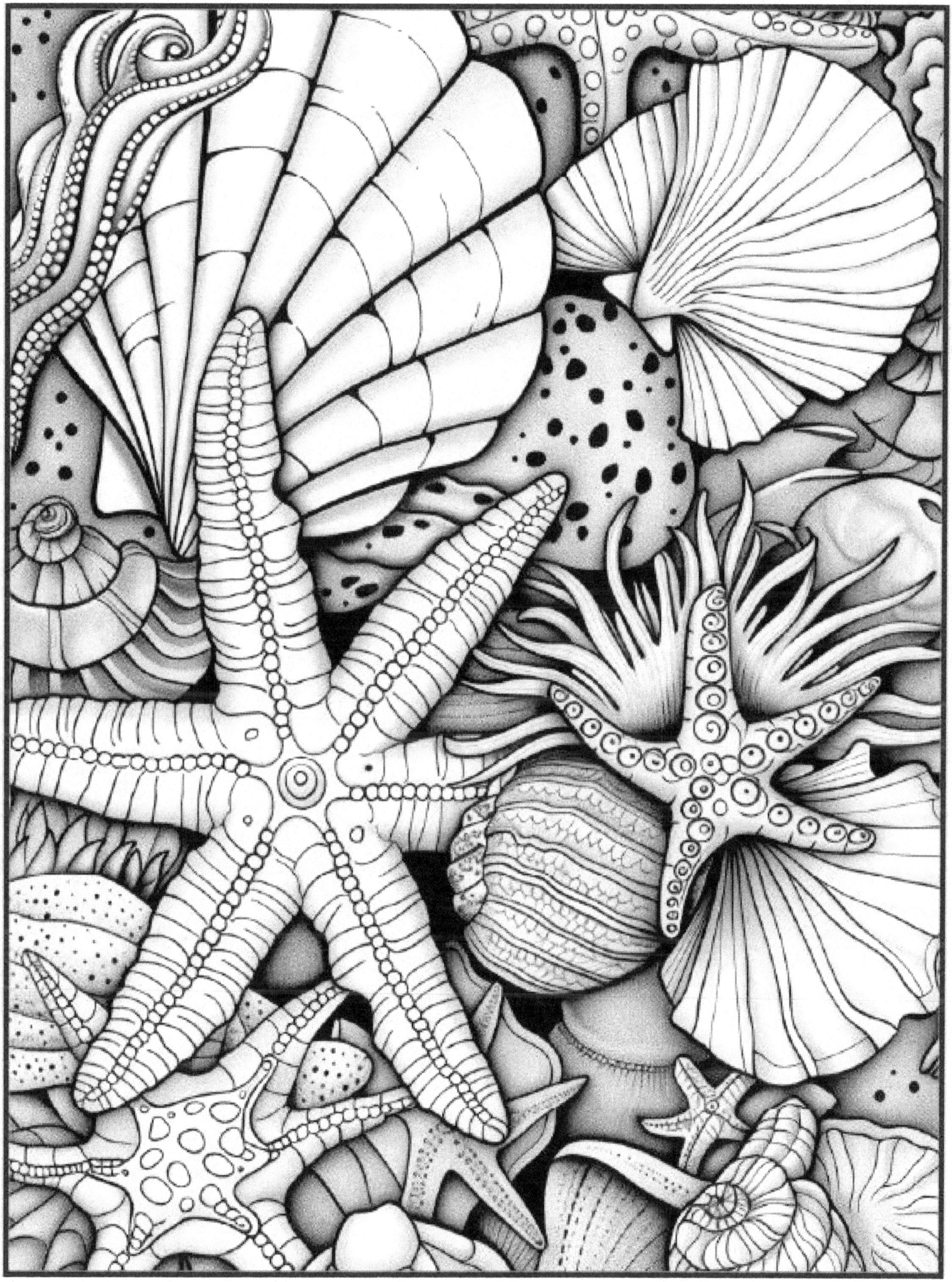

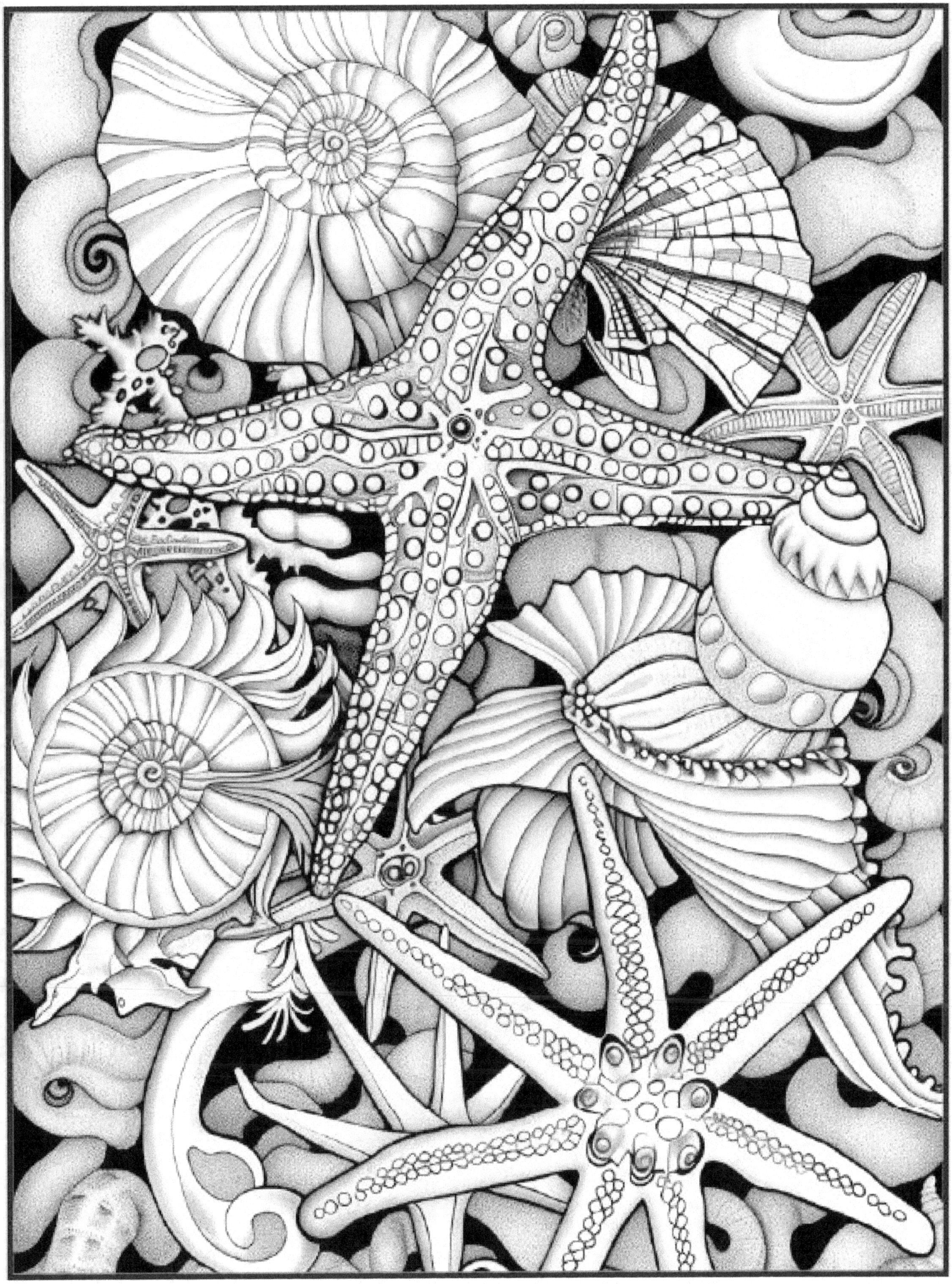

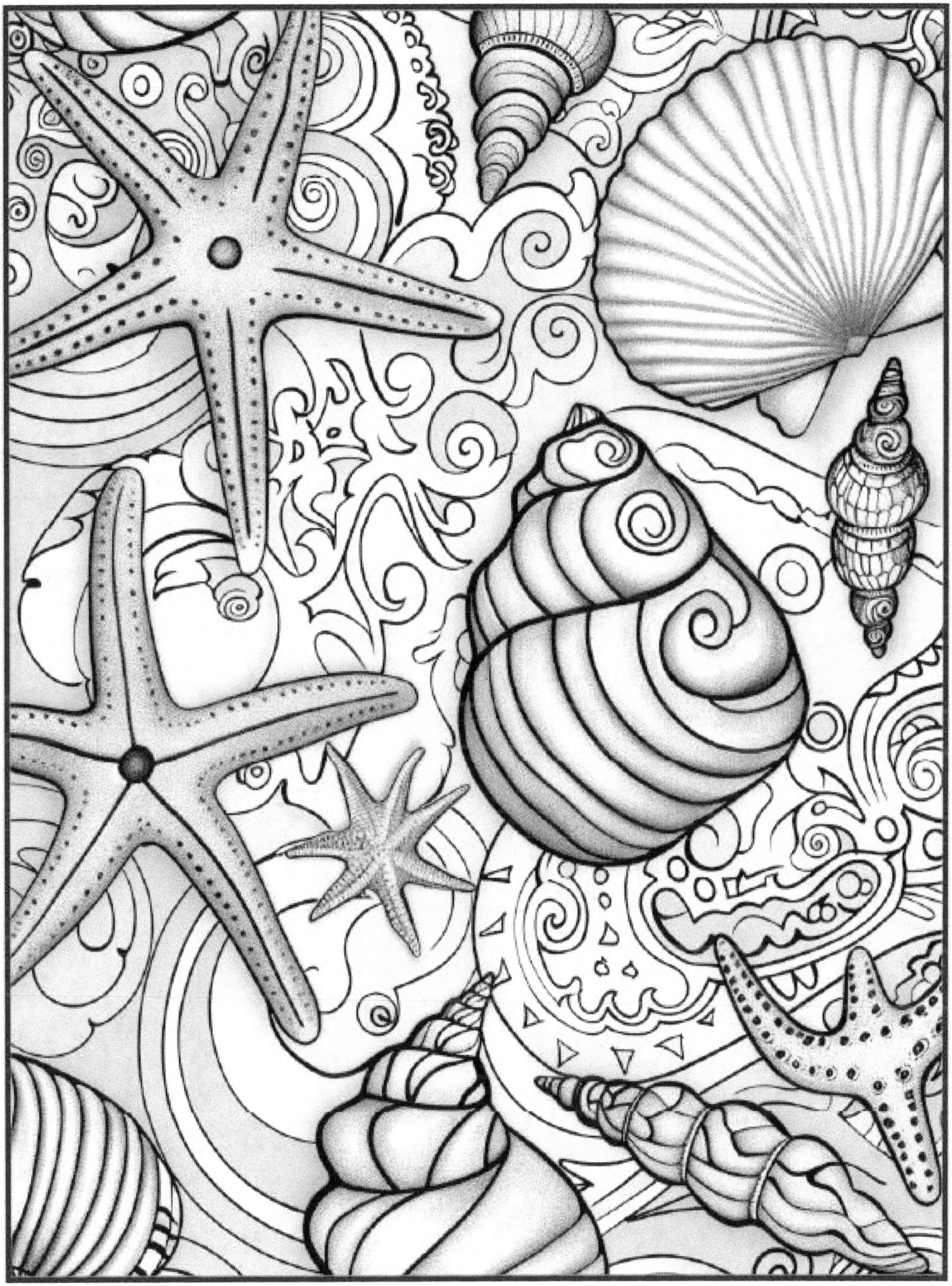

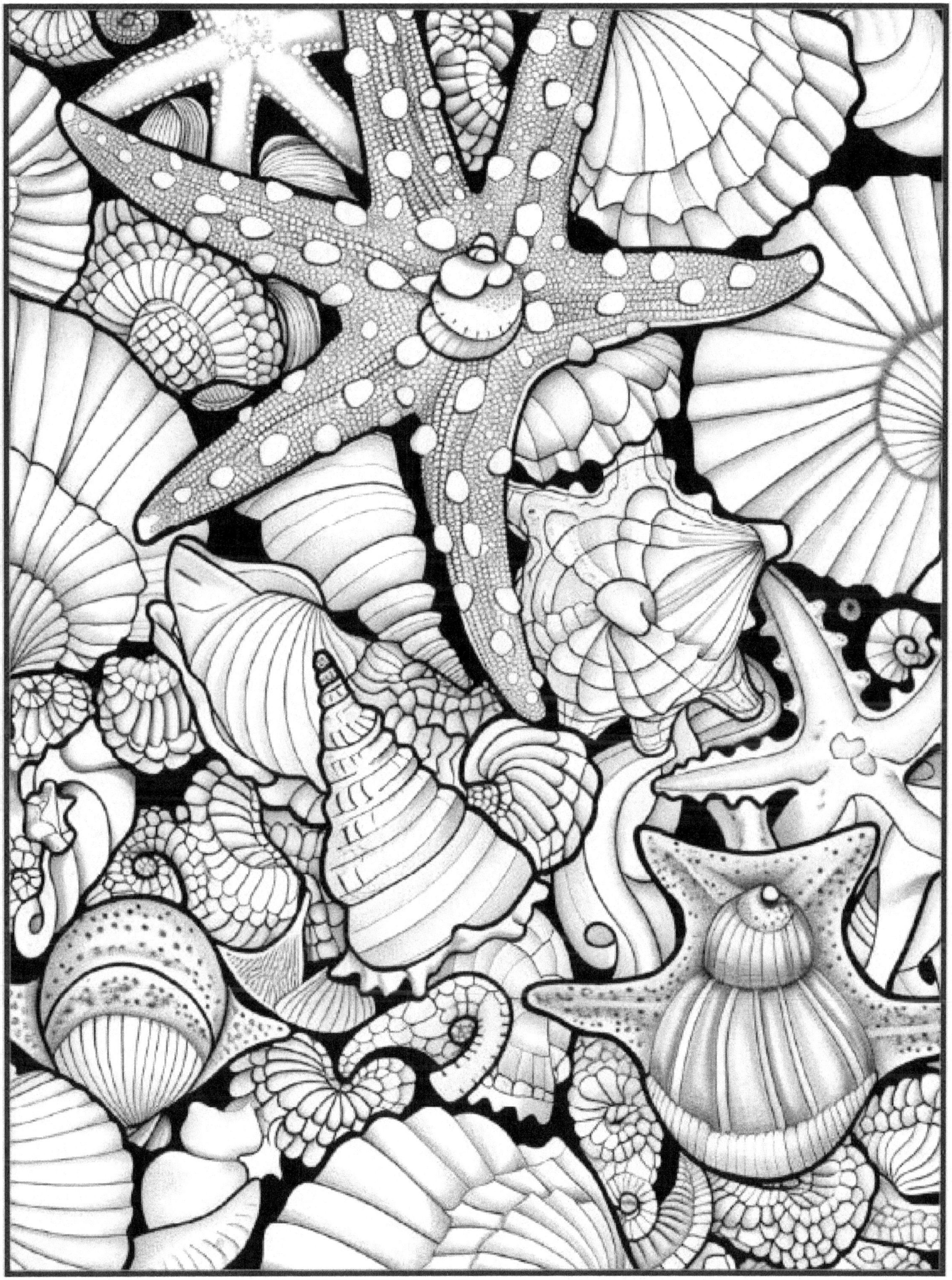

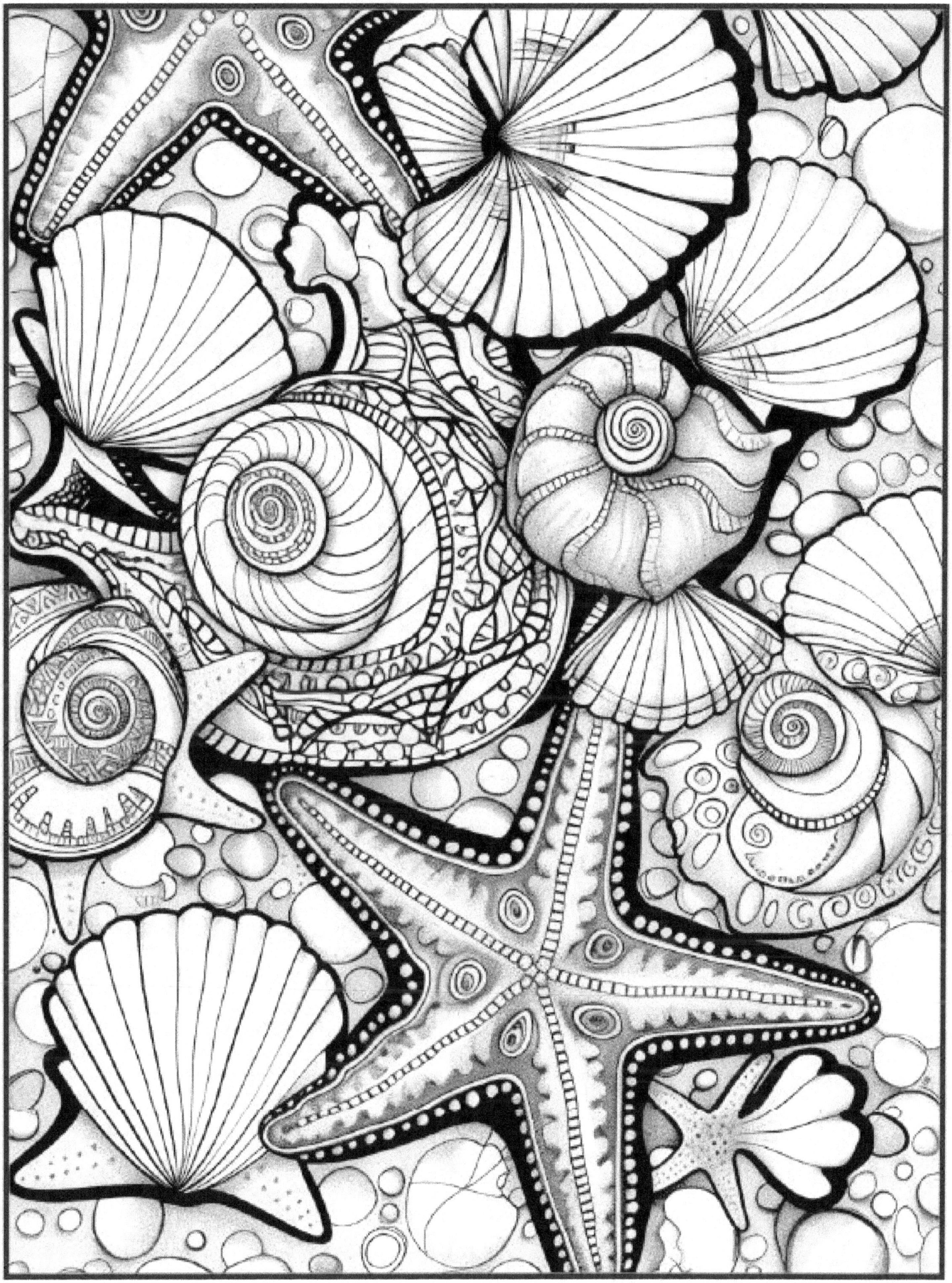

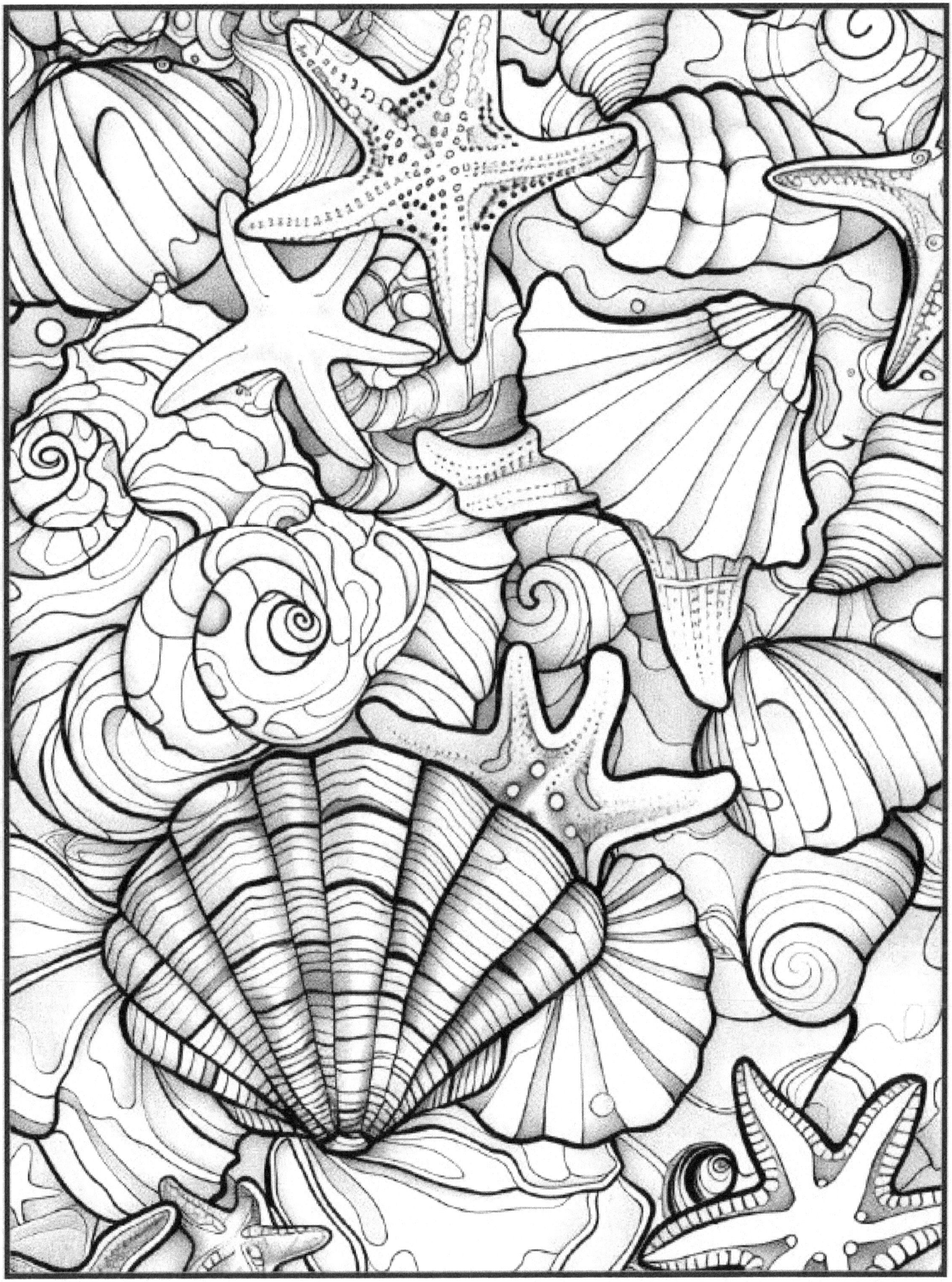

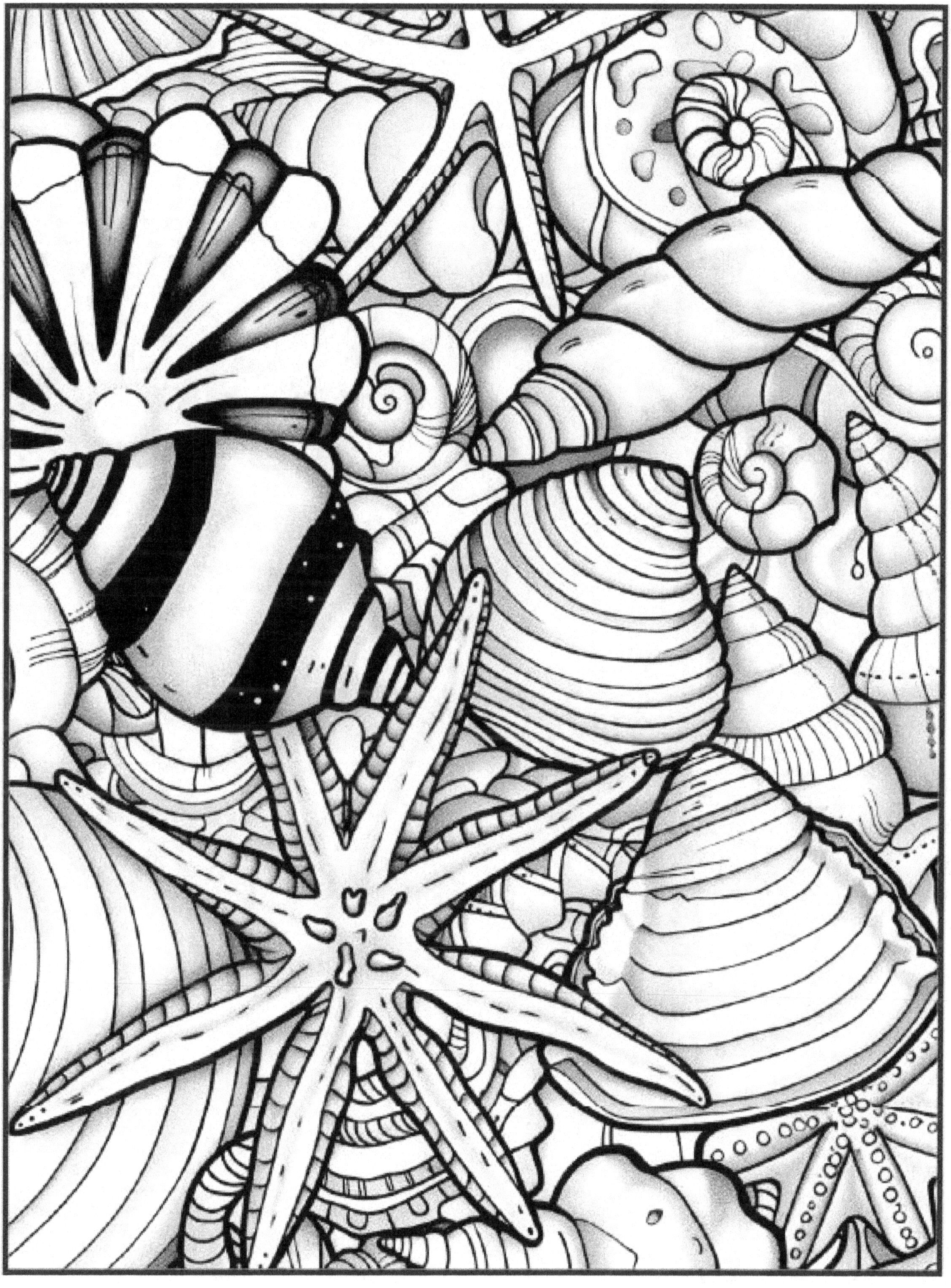

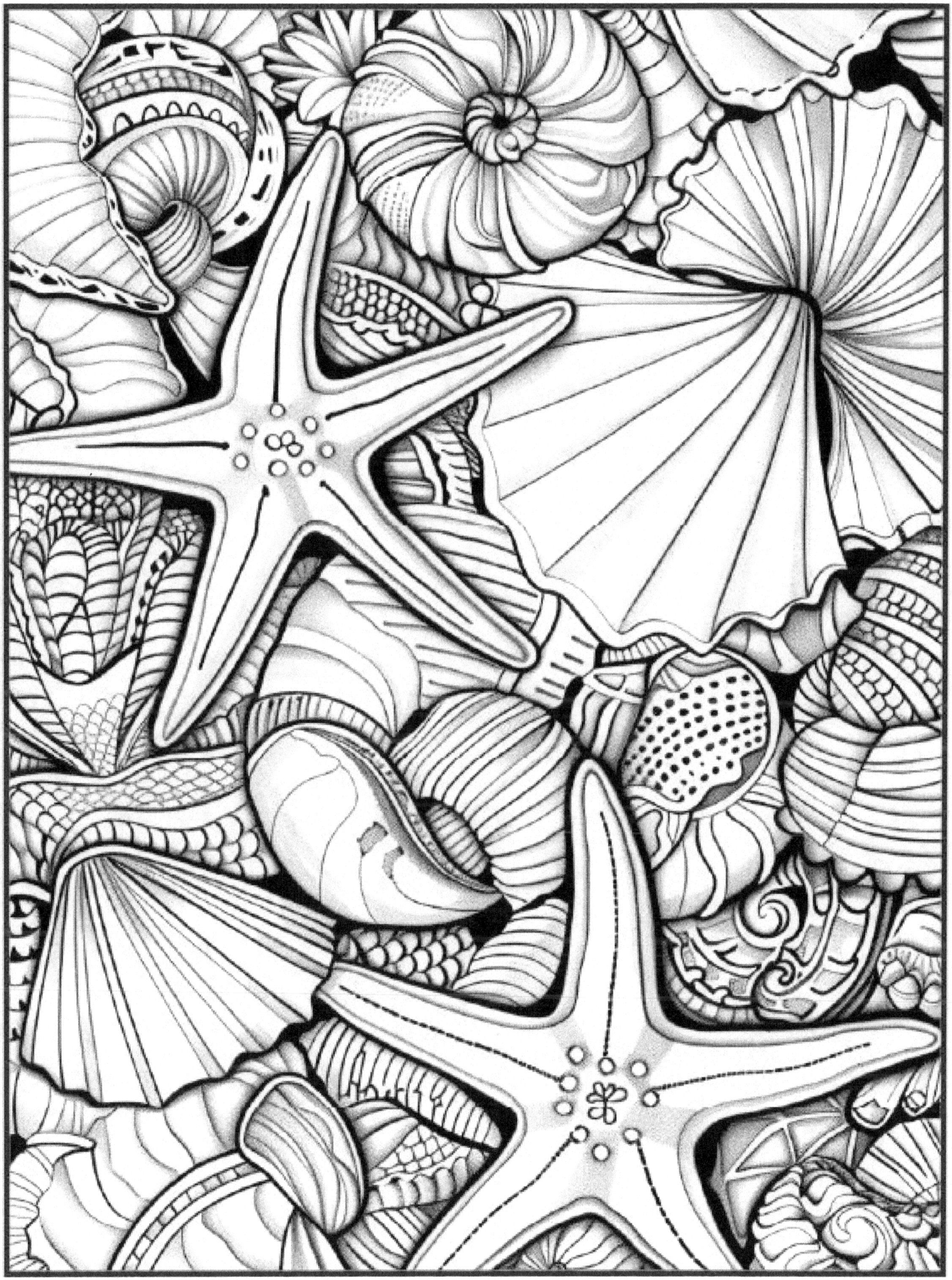

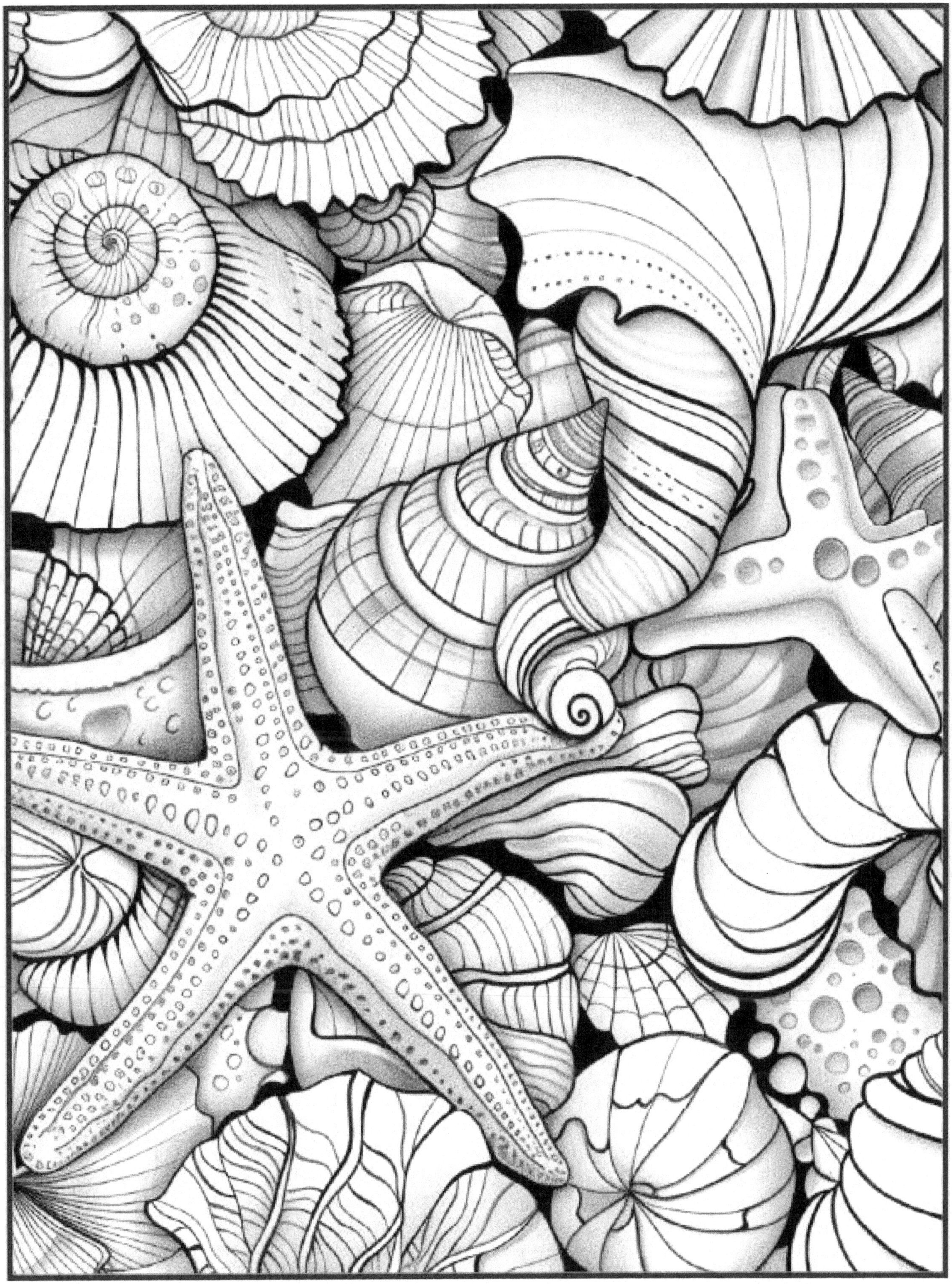

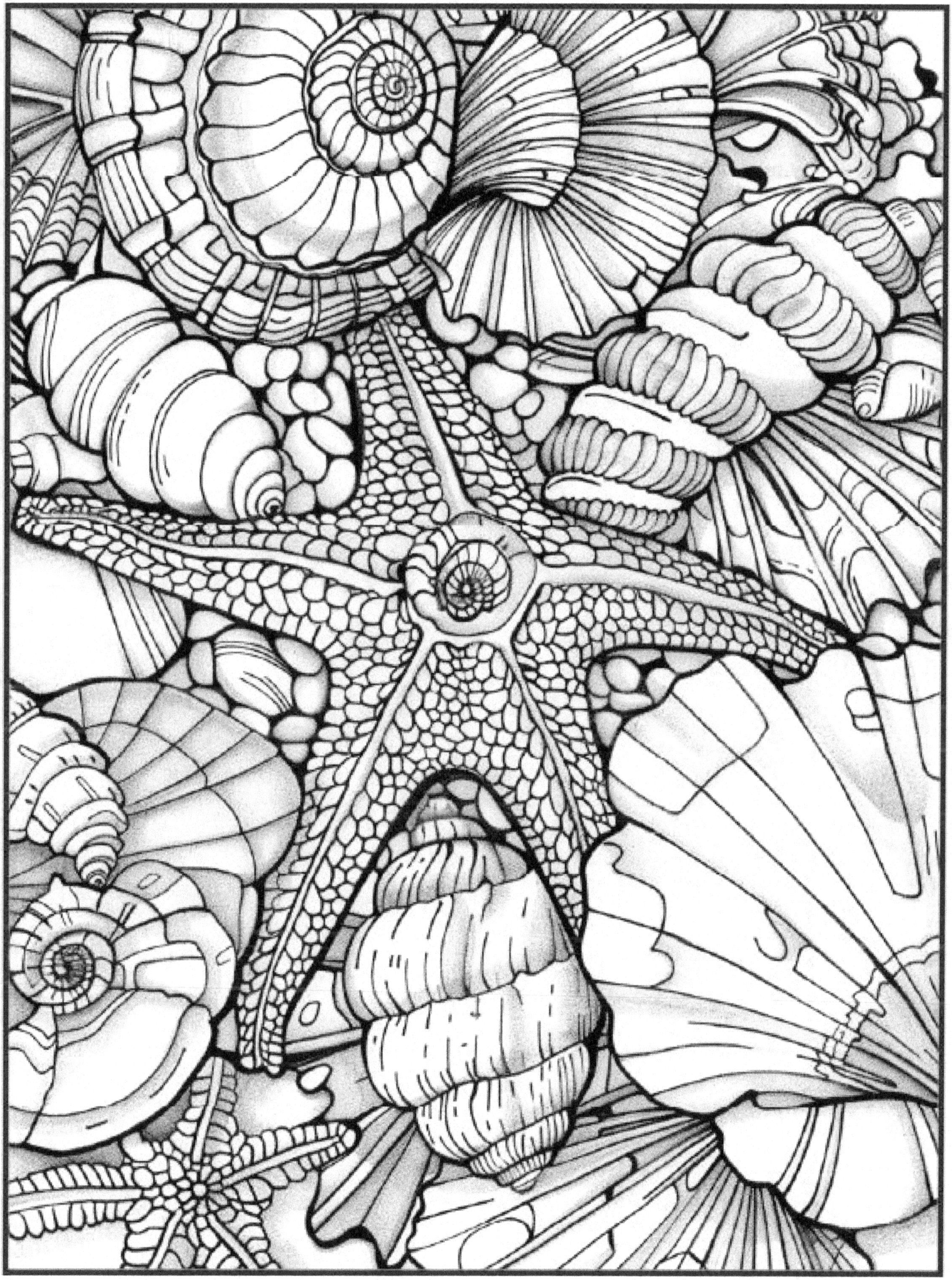

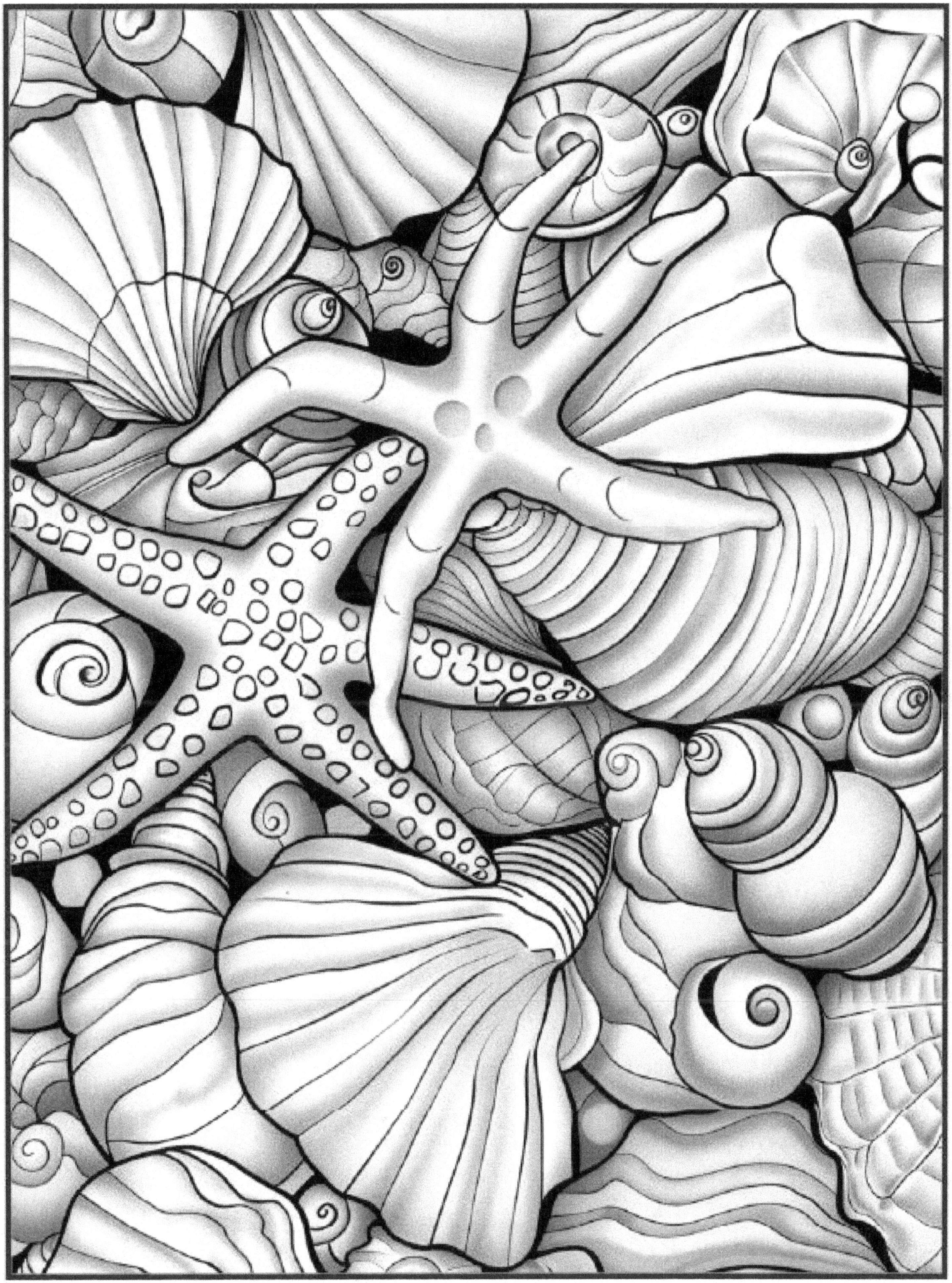

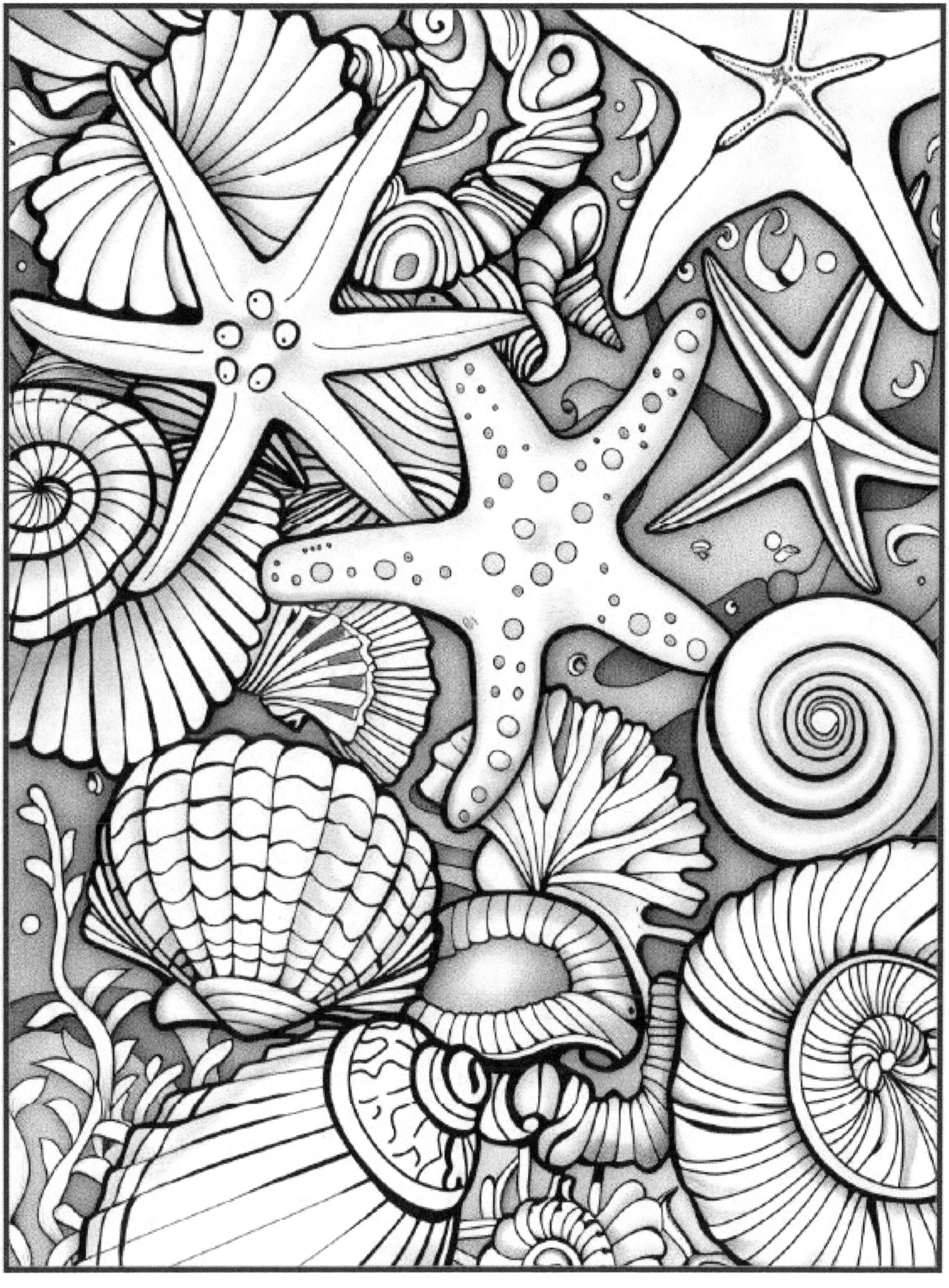

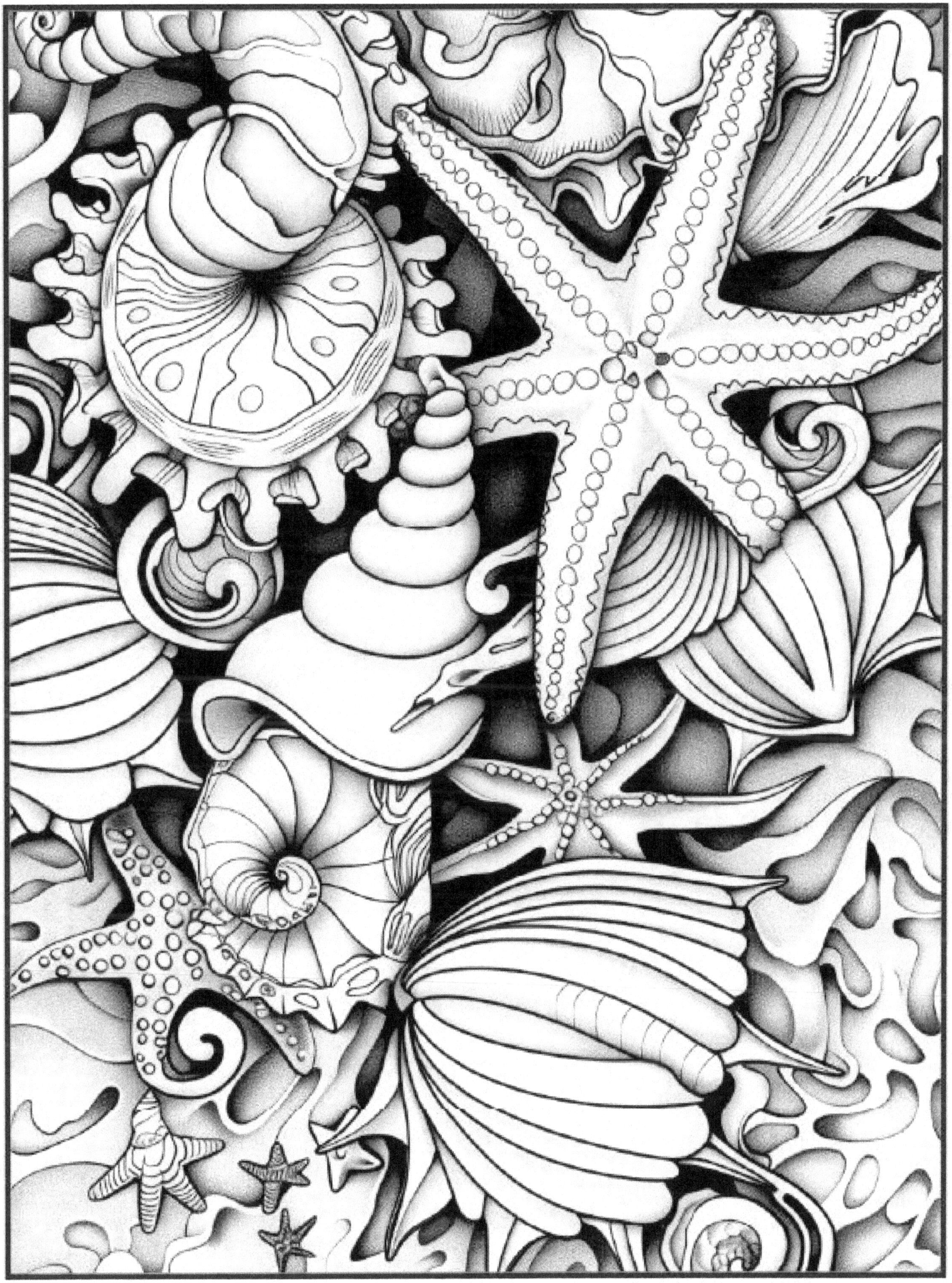

Thank you

PLEASE LEAVE US A REVIEW!

SCAN HERE

IF YOU ENJOYED THIS COLORING BOOK, PLEASE TAKE A MOMENT TO LEAVE A REVIEW. YOUR FEEDBACK HELPS US IMPROVE AND GUIDES OTHER CREATIVE SPIRITS TO THEIR PERFECT COLORING ADVENTURE!

FOR MORE CREATIVE COLORING BOOKS, PLEASE SEARCH FOR COLORQUEST COLLECTIONS IN YOUR FAVORITE BOOKSTORE!

COLORQUEST COLLECTIONS

COLORQUEST COLLECTIONS

www.ingramcontent.com/pod-product-compliance
Lightning Source LLC
Chambersburg PA
CBHW082345220526
45470CB00008B/2653
* 9 7 9 8 3 2 6 9 1 2 7 0 1 *